Praise for *Building AI-Powered Products*

Marily Nika has written the handbook for product leaders navigating this time of change brought on by AI. Her insights on leveraging AI as a tool will change how we build. Rather than making products less personal, she shows how AI can make our work more meaningful and transformative.

—*Deb Liu, president and CEO, Ancestry.com*

Marily says that all PMs will be AI PMs, and I believe it. This book is the guide to get there. She provides a blend of frameworks, case studies, and practical advice to help you transition your career and build successful products powered by AI.

—*Lenny Rachitsky, author,* Lenny's Newsletter, *and podcast host*

In a time when AI is reshaping industries at an unprecedented pace, Marily Nika's book provides the essential frameworks and insights that product managers need to lead with confidence and stay ahead. This timely guide sets the foundation for success in the AI-driven future, as experienced by students of Marily's course offered on Maven.

—*Gagan Biyani, CEO and cofounder, Maven Learning, Inc.*

T0319599

In a world full of AI noise, Marily offers a refreshing and pragmatic take on what it takes to build products with AI. If you are a PM, this is an essential read. It is filled with practical frameworks and tools that you can apply right away.

—*Amit Fulay, vice president of product, Microsoft*

Marily Nika's book arrives at a pivotal moment in the evolution of AI and product management. Her deep expertise and practical frameworks provide invaluable guidance for leaders aiming to leverage AI's transformative potential. This work is a significant contribution to the field.

—*Karim R. Lakhani, professor of business administration and chair, Digital, Data, and Design Institute, Harvard University*

Building AI-Powered Products

*The Essential Guide to AI and
GenAI Product Management*

Dr. Marily Nika

Building AI-Powered Products

by Dr. Marily Nika

Copyright © 2025 Marily Nika. All rights reserved.

Published by O'Reilly Media, Inc., 1005 Gravenstein Highway North, Sebastopol, CA 95472.

O'Reilly books may be purchased for educational, business, or sales promotional use. Online editions are also available for most titles (*http://oreilly.com*). For more information, contact our corporate/institutional sales department: 800-998-9938 or *corporate@oreilly.com*.

Acquisitions Editor: David Michelson	**Indexer:** BIM Creatives, LLC
Development Editor: Sarah Grey	**Interior Designer:** Monica Kamsvaag
Production Editor: Elizabeth Faerm	**Cover Designer:** Susan Thompson
Copyeditor: Audrey Doyle	**Illustrator:** Kate Dullea
Proofreader: Vanessa Moore	

February 2025: First Edition

Revision History for the First Edition

2025-02-14: First Release

See *http://oreilly.com/catalog/errata.csp?isbn=9781098152703* for release details.

The O'Reilly logo is a registered trademark of O'Reilly Media, Inc. *Building AI-Powered Products*, the cover image, and related trade dress are trademarks of O'Reilly Media, Inc.

The views expressed in this work are those of the author and do not represent the publisher's views. While the publisher and the author have used good faith efforts to ensure that the information and instructions contained in this work are accurate, the publisher and the author disclaim all responsibility for errors or omissions, including without limitation responsibility for damages resulting from the use of or reliance on this work. Use of the information and instructions contained in this work is at your own risk. If any code samples or other technology this work contains or describes is subject to open source licenses or the intellectual property rights of others, it is your responsibility to ensure that your use thereof complies with such licenses and/or rights.

978-1-098-15270-3

[LSI]

Contents

Preface

Artificial intelligence (AI) has been a core area of research and development for computer scientists and engineers for decades. While the potential of AI remained constrained by hardware and software for years, recent breakthroughs have allowed product managers to harness AI's power, scaling it into practical and impactful solutions.

In 2023, the launch of OpenAI's ChatGPT and similar large language models transformed the landscape of digital products, empowering product managers to infuse AI into user experiences in ways that were unimaginable just a year before. In the span of a year, the market has seen a Cambrian explosion of generative AI models, from image generation tools like Midjourney, Stable Diffusion, and DALL-E to advanced search solutions like Deepseek—and even multimodal AI systems like Google's Gemini. As of 2024, most tech companies are focused on integrating some aspect of AI into their products, with many prioritizing the transition from task-specific AI solutions to general-purpose AI and building new user experiences with multimodal AI and personalized AI agents.

Building AI-Powered Products: The Essential Guide to AI and GenAI Product Management is a road map for navigating the complexities of creating AI-driven products. Drawing on my experiences at Google and Meta, and complemented by insights from the AI Product Academy, this guide aims to equip product managers, entrepreneurs, and business leaders with the tools and frameworks to confidently integrate AI into their work.

Why AI Product Management?

AI product management is uniquely challenging. Unlike traditional product development, AI systems are probabilistic, depend on high-quality data, and demand continuous learning and optimization. Concepts such as large language models, retrieval-augmented generation, and model fine-tuning are critical to understand, yet they often feel inaccessible to nontechnical PMs. This is why I founded the AI Product Academy, which provides AI Product Management certifications, and it is the reason I wrote this book: to bridge the gap between niche AI technologies and solve user pain points in impactful ways. The book offers actionable guidance, practical tools, and case studies to help you navigate the intricate AI Product Development Lifecycle, tackle strategic and ethical considerations, and build products that are both innovative and user centric.

Who Should Read This Book?

This book is for product leaders of all levels who want to learn how to manage, build, and land AI and generative AI-powered products as well as AI product organizations. I have designed the content to be relevant to different audiences, from technical professionals eager to explore AI's possibilities, to business leaders looking to staff their own organizations with AI product leaders and gain a competitive edge. Approximately 8,000 professionals have taken my AI PM Bootcamp to date, and most of them fall into these three categories:

Seasoned product leaders
   Staffing and leading AI product organizations

Product managers
   Transitioning to AI or refining their skills to manage AI-powered products

Entrepreneurs and innovators
   Exploring AI's potential to transform their businesses

Engineers and data scientists
   Understanding product- and user-focused aspects of AI development

What This Book Covers

AI is not the product; the experience is the product. To bring value to users, AI needs to be integrated into an experience, enhancing it or contributing to solving an unmet need. This book is for building AI and generative AI experiences, from ideation to rollout. It is absolutely critical for anyone looking to collaborate with technical teams to bring AI products to life.

This book is structured to guide you through every stage of building AI-powered products, from initial ideation to market deployment:

Chapter 1, "The Role of AI Product Managers"
  Explains the unique responsibilities of AI product managers and their role in translating technical advancements into user-driven solutions

Chapter 2, "The AI Product Development Lifecycle"
  Introduces the AI Product Development Lifecycle framework to systematically guide products through ideation, prototyping, testing, and deployment

Chapter 3, "Essential AI PM Knowledge"
  Covers essential AI concepts, including the AI lifecycle and fundamentals of AI algorithms and how they translate into user impacting features

Chapter 4, "The AI PM's Day-to-Day"
  Discusses the unique workflow of an AI product manager, highlighting the collaborative aspects, diverse stakeholders, and continuous learning required to succeed

Chapter 5, "Strategic Thinking in AI"
  Offers strategies for leading diverse teams of engineers, designers, and stakeholders

Chapter 6, "Setting Goals and Measuring Success"
  Explores how to define success metrics, balance trade-offs such as accuracy versus speed, and manage AI-specific risks

Chapter 7, "AI Tools for Product Managers "
  Highlights the tools and technologies that are critical throughout the AI Product Development Lifecycle

Chapter 8, "Building AI Agents"
  Delves into autonomous AI agents, exploring multi-agent systems, reinforcement learning, and practical applications in real-world products

O'Reilly Online Learning

O'REILLY® For more than 40 years, *O'Reilly Media* has provided technology and business training, knowledge, and insight to help companies succeed.

Our unique network of experts and innovators share their knowledge and expertise through books, articles, and our online learning platform. O'Reilly's online learning platform gives you on-demand access to live training courses, in-depth learning paths, interactive coding environments, and a vast collection of text and video from O'Reilly and 200+ other publishers. For more information, visit *https://oreilly.com*.

How to Contact Us

Please address comments and questions concerning this book to the publisher:

O'Reilly Media, Inc.

1005 Gravenstein Highway North

Sebastopol, CA 95472

800-889-8969 (in the United States or Canada)

707-827-7019 (international or local)

707-829-0104 (fax)

support@oreilly.com

https://oreilly.com/about/contact.html

We have a web page for this book, where we list errata, examples, and any additional information. You can access this page at *https://oreil.ly/bldg-ai-pwrd-prdcts*.

For news and information about our books and courses, visit *https://oreilly.com*.

Find us on LinkedIn: *https://linkedin.com/company/oreilly-media*.

Watch us on YouTube: *https://youtube.com/oreillymedia*.

Acknowledgments

I would like to thank my husband, Ray, for his unwavering support throughout this journey. My gratitude also goes to Professor Karim R. Lakhani, whose encouragement led me to first explore teaching in 2018, and Jessie Li, whose research assistance was invaluable in shaping this book.

Closing Thoughts

All product managers will be AI product managers in the future. AI and generative AI empower us to solve problems and scale solutions in ways that were unimaginable just a decade ago. As you navigate this book, I hope it equips you with the knowledge, frameworks, and confidence to build impactful AI-powered products that align with user needs and business goals.

—DR. MARILY NIKA

The Role of AI Product Managers

The first AI team I ever worked for was designing something special: smart home–assistant devices that could understand a wide variety of accents, and even recognize who was talking and what they were instructing the assistant to do. It was the early days of voice assistants and smart homes. I had always been interested in the conjunction of language and tech, and I knew many voice systems didn't really "get" different ways of speaking. The Speech team's goal was to make an AI that did.

That was a really complicated task. We wrangled enormous datasets, refined algorithms, and spent months trying to figure out how to embed this technology into user-facing products. Speech technologies, and more specifically, speech recognition (*https://oreil.ly/GebkV*), enables machines to transcribe what humans are saying. Similarly, text-to-speech synthesis (*https://oreil.ly/7MPDk*) gives computers the ability to "speak," given written words as an input.

I didn't realize at first that I had found myself at the heart of AI and innovation. This experience showed me the exciting world of AI product management.

The field of AI has existed for many decades. It originated back in the 1950s (*https://oreil.ly/4MEqd*), when scientists attempted to develop computers that would emulate the way human brains work, and in particular when Alan Turing suggested that machines can also be taught to reason, just like humans.

AI is a field of computer science that gives computers intelligence. It enables machines to perform nontrivial cognitive tasks comparable to tasks humans can perform, such as reasoning, sensing, speech processing, visual perception, problem-solving, and most importantly, as Oracle notes (*https://oreil.ly/Or9Wx*), learning from data and adapting. While AI is not new (*https://oreil.ly/Bwv67*), hardware limitations had obscured its potential until recently. The industry is only now starting to unlock the vast potential of AI, a breakthrough made possible by leaps in chip technology, unprecedented computational power, and an abundance of data. These advancements, coupled with sophisticated algorithms and cutting-edge machine learning (ML) techniques, are setting the stage for AI to reach capabilities that were previously unimaginable.

Organizations with vast amounts of data are in a unique position to embrace AI and ML. They stand to gain a significant competitive advantage, both in their operations (e.g., predictions that inform planning, such as for restocking inventories or identifying the right price point) and in their offerings (unique, smart solutions that offer personalization, recommendations, automation, content generation, and more). Now more than ever, those organizations need professionals who can understand AI and its potential, leverage it, and "serve" it to customers.

Today, AI is ubiquitous. It drives increasingly complex and consequential decisions, such as college admissions and medical diagnoses. I write this in 2024, and in the past year alone, AI has advanced tremendously with the emergence of *generative AI*, a subtype of AI that produces content, sometimes abbreviated as "GenAI."

This chapter introduces the business role of the AI product manager (AI PM). I'll discuss what distinguishes this role from regular product management and what skill sets it requires. We'll also explore the diverse landscape of AI, including how AI products leverage different AI technologies, to give you a comprehensive view of both the day-to-day work lives of AI PMs and the broader context in which they operate.

The Stages of AI Evolution

GenAI is often conflated with traditional AI, but in reality, it's just one subset of a larger, more complex AI landscape. This distinction is crucial to understanding AI's full potential, yet it's a misconception I encounter daily. While GenAI has become a hot topic and the technology has made remarkable strides recently, it is by no means a replacement for traditional AI.

When we talk about "AI," it's important to clarify that this term encompasses a range of technologies and approaches, each with its own specific set of use cases. To assume that "AI" *just* refers to GenAI oversimplifies a vast, multifaceted field. Modern-day AI is classified into four groups: traditional, generative, general intelligence, and superintelligence.

Figure 1-1 highlights how these four types of AI vary in scope and capability, illustrating an evolving landscape where AI ranges from specialized tasks to broader, potentially transformative applications. The diagram emphasizes the layered complexity of AI, showing how each category contributes uniquely to our understanding and advancement of intelligent systems.

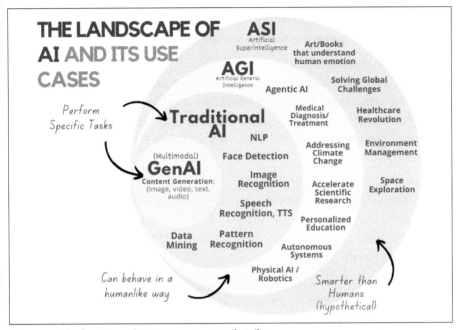

Figure 1-1. The four types of AI (source: Dr. Marily Nika)

TRADITIONAL AI (1950S–PRESENT)

Traditional AI has a long history that began in the 1950s and represents AI's foundational technologies. These systems are designed to perform specific tasks through rule-based or pattern recognition systems. Traditional AI includes some of the most essential applications we interact with on a daily basis:

Vision

Traditional AI has made strides in computer vision tasks such as image recognition, object detection, and face recognition. These technologies enable systems to interpret and analyze visual inputs, forming the basis for everything from photo tagging on social media platforms to advanced medical imaging technologies that help doctors diagnose diseases.

Speech

Speech recognition and speech-to-text technologies, such as those used in voice assistants like Siri and Alexa, have been in development for decades. These technologies convert spoken language into text, enabling machines to respond to voice commands. Text-to-speech (TTS) systems, which do the reverse, give computers the ability to speak in a humanlike manner.

Natural language processing (NLP)

NLP tasks such as language translation, sentiment analysis, and other tasks using chatbots have brought significant breakthroughs. Think of Google Translate or chatbots used in customer service; these rely on AI to understand human language in a more sophisticated way than simple keyword recognition.

Robotics

Traditional AI in robotics has led to the development of industrial robots, autonomous vehicles, and drones. These robots can perform complex tasks such as assembly in manufacturing plants or navigating streets autonomously.

Data analysis

Traditional AI excels in predictive analytics, data mining, and pattern recognition. It can analyze vast datasets and uncover hidden patterns, allowing organizations to make data-driven decisions and automate processes that once required human intuition.

GENERATIVE AI (LATE 2010S–PRESENT)

GenAI represents the more recent wave of AI innovation and has captivated the public's attention with its ability to create content. This content can be text, images, video, or even music, but GenAI does not replace the tasks handled by traditional AI. Instead, it opens up new dimensions:

Content creation

The ability to generate media such as images, video, and text from a given prompt is one of GenAI's core strengths. Applications range from creative arts (helping artists design graphics or write music) to business (automatically generating product descriptions for ecommerce websites).

Deepfakes

GenAI can also be used to create synthetic media, sometimes known as *deepfakes*, which can convincingly mimic real people's voices or appearances. While this technology raises ethical concerns, it also has legitimate applications in entertainment and simulation environments.

Personalized media

GenAI is being used to tailor content experiences to individuals. Platforms such as Netflix and Spotify are using AI to suggest shows and music that align with user preferences. This trend is reshaping media consumption, making it more personalized than ever before.

Design and art

AI tools such as DALL-E (*https://oreil.ly/MzMRb*) and Adobe Firefly (*https://oreil.ly/F4T-4*) assist artists in generating concepts or mockups. These tools reduce the time to produce creative work, empowering artists to focus on refining their ideas.

Game development

GenAI is making games more interactive and dynamic by allowing game developers to create procedurally generated worlds, characters, and environments, making each player's experience unique.

ARTIFICIAL GENERAL INTELLIGENCE (2030S?)

Artificial general intelligence (AGI) is the next frontier in AI research, and while we are not there yet, it holds the promise of machines capable of understanding, learning, and applying knowledge across a wide range of tasks—essentially mimicking human cognitive functions:

Problem-solving

AGI will be able to tackle complex, multidomain problems. Imagine AI systems capable of medical diagnosis one moment and strategic business planning the next.

Research and development

In R&D, AGI could dramatically accelerate scientific discovery by generating hypotheses, running simulations, and performing experiments much faster than humans can.

Personal assistants
> AGI could evolve today's virtual assistants into highly capable systems that can manage vast areas of daily life, from personal schedules to creative problem-solving.

Healthcare
> AGI will likely make huge strides in healthcare, offering personalized medicine, diagnosing complex conditions, and even proposing novel treatments.

ARTIFICIAL SUPERINTELLIGENCE (~2040S?)

Artificial superintelligence (ASI), while currently hypothetical, would surpass human intelligence, providing solutions to problems that are not even within our conceptual grasp today:

Solving global challenges
> If ASI becomes a reality, it could provide revolutionary solutions to large-scale problems such as climate change, world hunger, and geopolitical conflicts. ASI could offer new strategies to solve humanity's most pressing problems.

Reliable foresight
> Many of the decisions people make today are data driven. For example, weather forecasts are made based on thousands of historical data points. With ASI, future forecasts, whether they're for predicting weather or predicting changes in market pricing, will be more accurate.

Advanced space exploration
> Space missions and, potentially, interstellar colonization could be powered by the analytical and creative capabilities of ASI, solving complex problems of propulsion, life support, and resource management.

Now that we've explored the theoretical potential of AGI and ASI, it's essential to understand how AI is currently leveraged in real-world products. AI is already transforming industries in profound ways, and as an AI PM, your role is central to making these technologies practical and valuable to users. Let's take a look at some examples of groundbreaking AI-powered products and how AI PMs play a crucial part in their development.

How Products Leverage AI

As an AI PM, you have the potential to transform your industry by helping your organization strategically "infuse" its products with AI to create value. To highlight the diversity of what AI PMs can work on, let's look at a few examples of real-world transformative, groundbreaking AI products—and the role of AI PMs in their creation.

Google Photos is an application that organizes and stores users' photos and videos: "a home for all your photos and videos, organized and brought to life," as Google describes it (*https://oreil.ly/IZ8vD*). That value proposition was almost certainly conceived by the team's AI PMs. What's more, its search functionality (*https://oreil.ly/EdesI*) makes it easy for you to search your content using basic keywords (e.g., "dog"), without the need to pretrain the model. Simply enter the keyword, and Google Photos searches across all your photos and brings up those that contain that keyword. This feature uses multiple AI-based smart technologies, including face recognition, object detection, and scene detection, to identify and search for specific people ("Steve"), objects ("cars"), and locations or situations (e.g., "forest" or "wedding").

AI PMs have also had an impact on the development of self-driving cars. Tesla's Full Self-Driving (FSD) beta (*https://oreil.ly/j8uKS*), for example, can navigate streets, change lanes safely, and even park on its own. It uses technologies such as reinforcement learning (*https://oreil.ly/qhvZk*), an ML technique in which a machine uses its own experiences to learn by trial and error, and computer vision (*https://oreil.ly/LjQhV*), which enables computers to derive meaningful information from images, videos, and other visual input.

Another team I worked on, Google's augmented reality (AR)/virtual reality (VR) team, is developing Google Lens (*https://lens.google*). This technology helps users understand the world around them. It analyzes everything their camera is pointing to and enables actions—for example, live translation on-screen, personalized shopping recommendations, live reviews of a restaurant, and so on. The technologies it uses include computer vision and NLP, an AI tool that helps computers understand words (in speech or written text) in similar ways to humans.

From launching AI-powered photo organization tools to self-driving cars and augmented reality apps, AI PMs are at the forefront of some of the most exciting developments in tech. But what makes these technologies truly innovative goes beyond just the applications: they are built on the unique characteristics of AI itself. Understanding these foundational features is key to unlocking the full potential of AI-driven products.

Now, let's dive into what makes AI so distinct. Whether it's the way AI models learn, adapt, or handle uncertainty, these unique features shape how you approach product development, decision making, and UX design. Let's explore these features and how they impact your role as an AI PM.

Unique Features of AI

AI has several distinctive characteristics that set it apart from traditional software and other technological tools. Understanding these unique features is crucial as you navigate your role as an AI PM. These features not only shape how AI systems function, but also impact your decision making, prioritization, and the user experiences you design. Let's explore these features in depth, and I'll explain what each means for you and how they influence the products you create.

PROBABILISTIC NATURE

AI models operate based on probabilities rather than certainties. Unlike traditional software, which executes predefined commands and follows deterministic rules, AI makes predictions based on patterns it has learned from data. For example, an AI system might predict with 80% certainty that an image contains a dog, but there's still a 20% chance it could be something else entirely.

You need to embrace and manage uncertainty. You'll never have 100% certainty with AI predictions, so part of your role will be to set the right expectations with stakeholders and users. Understanding the trade-offs between accuracy and other product factors such as speed or cost is key. In applications such as self-driving cars, healthcare diagnostics, and financial trading, even small errors can have major consequences, so continuously improving model accuracy becomes a critical part of your road map. We dive deep into trade-offs in Chapter 3.

What helps me manage this uncertainty is setting up feedback loops to consistently monitor model performance and make adjustments, and to make sure the team has strategies for model retraining, testing, and refinement. More importantly, I make sure to define interfaces that reflect the probabilistic nature of AI in smart ways; for example, with confidence scores, or with warnings when the system isn't certain.

DEPENDENCY ON DATA

AI systems thrive on data. The more relevant, high-quality data you have, the better your model will perform. However, not all data is created equal. Bias, noise, and irrelevance in your datasets can result in skewed or flawed AI outputs.

As an AI PM, your success depends heavily on the quality and quantity of the data your AI model is trained on. Data sourcing, cleansing, and validation need to be key parts of your workflow. Without good data, even the best algorithms will fail to deliver meaningful results. You'll also need to balance data privacy concerns with the desire to collect as much data as possible.

I de-risk this dependency by working closely with the research and data scientists to ensure that data pipelines are set up correctly and that datasets are continuously cleaned and updated. When working on AI products such as personalized recommendations or predictive analytics, you'll need to have a strategy for acquiring both historical and real-time data. Additionally, implementing privacy-preserving techniques such as differential privacy can help you collect data while protecting user anonymity.

MODEL DRIFT

Unlike traditional software that remains static unless manually updated, AI models learn and improve over time. This ability to continuously learn is one of AI's biggest advantages.

However, it also introduces challenges, particularly around managing updates and ensuring that learning doesn't introduce new biases or errors. You'll need to think of your AI product not as a "one-and-done" release, but as a continuously evolving system.

Each new dataset or user interaction offers the opportunity for your model to learn and improve. But this also means you need to plan for long-term maintenance, model retraining, and continuous delivery of updates. It helps to implement processes that allow for ongoing learning and improvement, such as regular model retraining schedules or active learning frameworks where the model can query for more information in cases of uncertainty. When designing user experiences, ensure that you provide a feedback mechanism so that users can correct the AI or provide additional context to improve future outcomes. Think of tools such as Google Maps, which asks users to confirm whether suggested locations are accurate and then feeds that feedback directly into the model for better predictions in the future.

THE NEED FOR MODEL INTERPRETABILITY AND EXPLAINABILITY

AI models, especially complex ones such as neural networks (*https://oreil.ly/ ndyOv*) and deep learning models (*https://oreil.ly/7oopf*), can be *opaque*, meaning they make predictions or decisions in ways that are difficult for humans to understand. This "black-box" nature of AI can create challenges, particularly when transparency and accountability are critical (such as in healthcare, finance, or legal contexts). You'll have to balance model performance with interpretability. While the most accurate models might be highly complex, they may not be explainable, which could be a problem in industries where users or regulators demand clarity on how decisions are made. The lack of transparency can also erode user trust, especially if users don't understand how or why an AI system reached a particular conclusion.

I invest in interpretable AI models where possible, or I use techniques such as SHAP (*https://oreil.ly/q-XxY*) and LIME (*https://oreil.ly/z83re*) to explain predictions from more complex models. For example, in a credit scoring AI, you might need to be able to explain why a particular loan was denied based on key factors, even if the underlying model is a black box. As an AI PM, you'll also want to ensure that your user interfaces provide clear, digestible explanations for users about how AI decisions are made.

AUTOMATED DECISION MAKING

One of AI's most powerful features is its ability to make decisions autonomously, without human intervention. This capability is transforming industries—whether it's automating customer support with chatbots, optimizing supply chains, or navigating autonomous vehicles.

While automation offers massive efficiency gains, it also shifts responsibility. As an AI product manager, you need to carefully think about where to draw the line between human and machine decision making. When do you hand over full control to the AI, and when is human oversight necessary? This can vary depending on the context; automated marketing recommendations might not need human review, but medical diagnoses or legal decisions probably will.

You may want to design systems that allow for human oversight where necessary. For instance, you might implement a "human-in-the-loop" approach, where AI makes recommendations but a human user makes the final decision. Additionally, always include fail-safes and escalation protocols, especially in high-stakes environments such as healthcare and finance, where errors can have significant consequences. We will take a deeper dive into this content in Chapter 3.

SCALABILITY

One of AI's key strengths is its ability to scale rapidly. Once an AI model is trained, it can make thousands of decisions per second, far exceeding human capabilities. However, scalability brings its own set of challenges, especially when it comes to infrastructure, performance optimization, and data handling. You need to think about infrastructure from the very beginning. As your AI product grows, so too will its data processing and computational needs. AI models are resource intensive, so ensuring that you have the right cloud infrastructure or on-premises hardware to scale efficiently is critical. At the same time, scalability isn't just about infrastructure. It's about maintaining performance as your model handles larger volumes of data or more diverse user inputs.

Plan for scalability from day one. Choose cloud platforms that can scale with your AI's needs, and ensure that your pipelines and data architecture can handle both current and future demands. You'll also want to prioritize model optimization techniques that allow your AI to maintain its performance without requiring exponential increases in resources.

HOW THESE UNIQUE FEATURES CAN IMPACT USER EXPERIENCE

Now that you've explored AI's unique features, you'll notice that all of these factors ultimately feed into the user experience. AI, when implemented correctly, can create highly personalized, adaptive, and seamless interactions that would be impossible with traditional software. However, understanding these unique characteristics will help you navigate the complexities and challenges they introduce, including the following:

Managing user expectations

AI's probabilistic nature means you need to be transparent with users about how AI works. For example, displaying confidence scores or providing explanations for recommendations can help build trust.

Building for adaptability

Because AI models learn and evolve, your product should also evolve. This creates a user experience that adapts to individual preferences over time, delivering more relevant and personalized interactions.

Prioritizing transparency

In certain sectors, users need to trust that AI is making decisions fairly and accurately. Clear communication about how decisions are made can enhance user experience by fostering trust and accountability.

Optimizing for efficiency

Automation allows for faster, more efficient user experiences. Whether it's a chatbot resolving customer queries or an AI suggesting personalized shopping recommendations, automation enhances user experience by reducing friction and increasing satisfaction.

Superpowers of AI and GenAI

AI has evolved into a suite of superpowers that empower products and services in ways previously unimaginable. From understanding and predicting user needs to automating workflows and generating new content, AI and GenAI open doors to experiences that are more personalized, creative, and efficient. Together, these technologies transform how users interact with products, offering unprecedented value and innovation. I've compiled a list of seven superpowers that AI products currently offer users. These are unique product features that directly impact how users interact with their environment.

SUPERPOWER 1: LEARNING FROM MASSIVE DATA AND CONTENT

One of AI's core strengths lies in its ability to learn from data. AI systems analyze vast amounts of user-generated content and past interactions to derive insights and make predictions. Whether it's recommending a new song on Spotify or predicting traffic patterns on Google Maps, AI's power to process large datasets enables businesses to provide users with relevant, timely information.

GenAI takes this even further by learning from massive amounts of user-generated content, digesting and synthesizing this data to generate new insights or outputs. For instance, it can predict user preferences based on previous behavior and even generate new suggestions or forecasts. In streaming services, this capability allows for ultra-personalized recommendations that reflect a user's tastes in real time, adjusting as their preferences evolve.

SUPERPOWER 2: PERSONALIZATION AT SCALE

AI's capacity to deliver tailored experiences to vast numbers of individuals is crucial for providing personalized services at scale. This technology enables recommendation platforms to offer each user a unique, customized experience. The power of AI extends beyond static recommendations by dynamically adapting to users' evolving preferences and behaviors in real time. For instance, Pinterest leverages this technology to craft design suggestions that align with an individual's changing aesthetic preferences.

What makes this scalable personalization especially impressive is the algorithm's ability to understand and categorize vast groups of people. By analyzing patterns and trends within large datasets, AI algorithms can discern common preferences and behaviors among groups, then fine-tune their recommendations for individual users based on how they relate to these larger segments. This dual understanding of both group dynamics and individual preferences allows AI to offer highly relevant, continually adaptive experiences at scale.

SUPERPOWER 3: AUTOMATING AND OPTIMIZING WORKFLOWS

AI has long been valued for its ability to automate workflows and routine tasks. Whether it's organizing schedules, managing emails, or tracking project progress, AI systems can offload tedious manual work, allowing users to focus on what truly matters.

GenAI takes workflow automation to the next level by not just automating tasks but also optimizing them based on real-time data. Imagine a GenAI assistant that schedules meetings while also analyzing team availability and project deadlines to optimize productivity. This level of automation allows businesses to offer smarter, more efficient tools that evolve alongside user needs.

SUPERPOWER 4: GENERATING NEW CONTENT AND EXPERIENCES

Traditionally, AI has been instrumental in automating workflows and optimizing processes. For example, task management systems such as Trello use AI to automate scheduling, track deadlines, and assist with project management. These AI capabilities help users focus on more meaningful tasks by automating routine activities.

However, *content generation* is where GenAI shines. With its capability to create text, images, and even video content, GenAI is revolutionizing creative industries. Tools such as ChatGPT and DALL-E allow businesses to generate written reports, visuals, and designs at scale, offering users new ways to interact with AI-generated content. A platform such as Adobe's generative design tool can produce graphics based on a user's brief, offering a level of creativity and flexibility that traditional automation tools can't match.

SUPERPOWER 5: PREDICTION AND FORECASTING

AI's predictive capabilities have long been a superpower for industries that rely on forecasting trends, inventory, or market behaviors. AI systems use historical data and user behavior to make informed predictions. Whether it's predicting future sales or anticipating market shifts, these capabilities allow businesses to stay ahead of the curve.

With GenAI, *predictive analytics* becomes even more powerful. GenAI systems can understand trends at a deeper level by processing vast and complex datasets. This capability enables more accurate predictions and, importantly, actionable insights that can directly influence decision making. For example, an AI-powered stock forecasting tool can predict market behavior while simultaneously generating strategies for action, enabling more intelligent decision making for users in real time.

SUPERPOWER 6: REAL-TIME ADAPTATION

AI has enabled real-time interactions, especially in voice and text interfaces such as Siri, Alexa, and customer service chatbots. These systems can process inputs instantly and offer users a level of immediacy in responses, which improves accessibility and convenience.

A fascinating superpower is GenAI's ability to *adapt on the fly*. GenAI can understand user inputs and deliver refined outputs in real time, allowing for dynamic, conversational interactions. For instance, an AI agent can provide real-time responses, adapting to the flow of a conversation and improving its relevance and accuracy as it gathers more context from the user's responses.

SUPERPOWER 7: UNLOCKING NEW TYPES OF USER EXPERIENCES WITH NEW FORM FACTORS

AI and GenAI are not only transforming digital environments, but also unlocking new possibilities through hardware advancements and emerging form factors. Devices such as smart glasses, VR headsets, and wearable technology are reshaping how users interact with AI-powered systems. These new form factors blend the physical and digital worlds, creating immersive, seamless experiences that were previously unimaginable.

The AI PM's Role

AI product management is a relatively new and very popular discipline that's all about turning AI research into real-world features and products. It's a rewarding job role that requires a diverse skill set. AI PMs bring AI expertise to the product strategy table and leverage one or many of the superpowers previously discussed to create innovative, strategic AI product road maps.

You're probably already familiar with the role of a product manager—let's refer to this as a "generalist PM." A generalist PM helps their team and company build and launch the right product by identifying user needs and aligning them with business goals. Think of an AI PM as a supercharged version of this role. An AI PM doesn't just ensure that the team is solving the right problem for the right user; they do so with a proactive, data-driven approach that leverages AI's unique capabilities to create personalized, intelligent experiences.

As an AI PM, you won't be expected to write code or train models. Your core focus will still be on designing world-class solutions to complex user problems. However, what sets you apart is your AI expertise, enabling you to identify where AI can add the most value, navigate its limitations and make strategic decisions regarding its trade-offs, and align AI capabilities with user needs in ways a generalist PM might not.

Figure 1-2 depicts where a generalist PM sits in most enterprises: at the intersection of business, research and development, and engineering. Generalist PMs are as much a part of the engineering team as the other teams are. Their job is to identify what users need, translate those needs into technical requirements, and help the engineers build and ship the product to users.

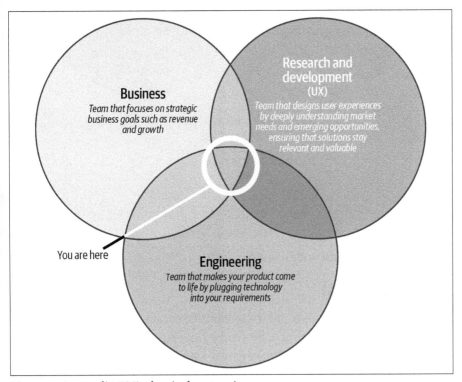

Business
Team that focuses on strategic business goals such as revenue and growth

Research and development
(UX)
Team that designs user experiences by deeply understanding market needs and emerging opportunities, ensuring that solutions stay relevant and valuable

You are here

Engineering
Team that makes your product come to life by plugging technology into your requirements

Figure 1-2. A generalist PM's place in the enterprise

AI PMs sit in that same intersection of departments, as Figure 1-3 shows. However, AI PMs can either be AI experiences PMs who enhance existing products with AI capabilities or AI builder PMs who work with the core technology first in order to explore entirely new solutions where users aren't yet defined. Both types of AI PMs must navigate the intricate landscape of AI technologies to discover and validate product–market fit, whether improving current user experiences or creating innovative features for potential future users.

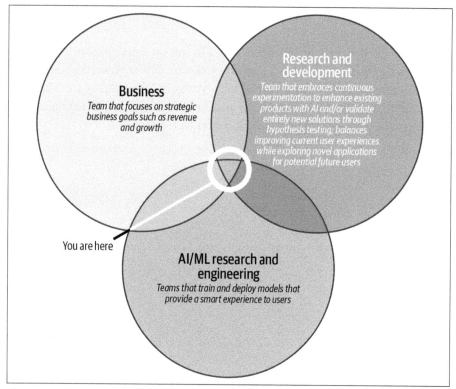

Figure 1-3. An AI PM's place in the enterprise

The AI PM's Skill Set

If business roles had recipes, the ingredient list for an AI PM would look like the combination in Figure 1-4: core product management craft and practices, engineering foundations for PMs, essential leadership and collaboration skills, and AI lifecycle and operational awareness.

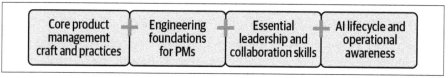

Figure 1-4. The different buckets of the AI PM skill set

Let's look at each one in turn:

Core product management craft and practices

This is the foundation every PM needs, regardless of their industry or product type. It includes understanding users' needs, setting a vision for a product, prioritizing features, and more. It's about the why and what of a product. Throughout this book, we'll dive deeper into what makes this general knowledge crucial for an AI PM.

Engineering foundations for PMs

Generalist PMs aren't usually required to have technical skills to get hired, although such skills are appreciated—some companies even have a technical interview loop as part of their hiring process. For AI PMs, however, some AI knowledge is usually required. While you might not be coding the product, understanding its technical aspects, including software development practices and tools, is invaluable. This knowledge bridges the gap between an AI PM and their technical team, ensures smoother communication, and helps set realistic expectations.

Essential leadership and collaboration skills

Often overlooked but immensely vital, these skills include effective communication, leadership, empathy, and creativity. These skills are instrumental in navigating challenges, fostering teamwork, and ensuring that the products you build will resonate with users. While they might sound intuitive, mastering them requires conscious effort. This book will offer guidance on honing these essential skills.

AI lifecycle and operational awareness

Perhaps most uniquely, an AI PM needs to grasp the nuances of AI, from ML algorithms to the intricacies of model training. This lets you:

- Understand what is and isn't possible with AI
- Identify and solve the right user problems
- Earn respect by communicating effectively with engineers and data scientists
- Be confident in making informed, strategic decisions, such as assessing the trade-offs of different algorithms or evaluating metrics to decide whether a product is ready to launch

- Assess the quality of your own features, and troubleshoot to catch and resolve bugs

Subsequent chapters will unpack each of these components in detail, ensuring that you're well equipped with a complete AI PM toolkit. Figure 1-5 gives you an idea of the many hats AI PMs wear.

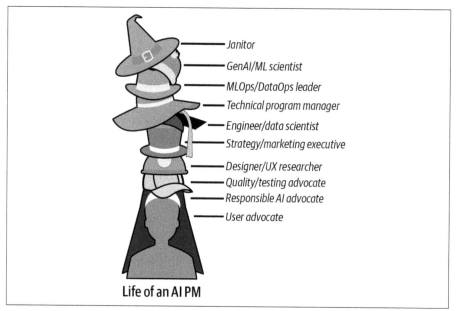

Figure 1-5. *The different hats of an AI PM*

Organizational Structures

An AI PM's place in the organizational and reporting structure varies significantly from company to company. The role is so new that many enterprises are still figuring out how best to align it with their overall business, product strategies, and goals. The factors that affect this decision include the company's size and stage (e.g., a Series A startup versus an organization with 1,000 employees), its long-term strategic goals for AI, its industry, its employees' level of technical expertise, and how well it is set up for cross-functional collaboration.

If the company does not have in-house technical expertise, the AI PM may report to a third-party agency. If AI is used widely across the company, however, there might be a centralized AI product management team. In earlier-stage startups, there's usually just one AI PM, often reporting directly to the CEO or chief technology officer (CTO). In more mature companies, AI PMs are more likely to report to a business-oriented leader, such as the vice president of product management.

Why Become an AI PM?

No child grows up wanting to be a product manager. Most of us don't discover that it's an option until we go to university or enter the workforce. People "stumble upon it" from all paths of life, and fall in love with its high-responsibility, high-reward nature.

Although AI PMs are a diverse group, if you're reading this, chances are good that you belong to one of three basic groups.

The first group is people who want to get into AI product management from a related field. You might already be very senior and leading product teams, and it might be time for your team to start leveraging AI. You might be a technical person who doesn't have much product management experience, or a generalist PM who wants to move into AI. This book will help you develop your skills and establish a career trajectory. You might worry that you're "too technical to be in Product" or "not technical enough for AI." Instead, your mindset should be: "I understand enough about AI. Users are my focus, and leveraging AI will allow me to ship great products for them."

The second group is AI enthusiasts who want to get into AI product management, such as recent graduates and professionals in entirely different fields. You can become an AI PM, and you're in the right place: this book will equip you with information you will find invaluable as you navigate the world of AI-powered products. The book discusses the intricacies of AI product management, demystifying complex concepts and making them accessible for everyone.

The third group is people looking to recruit, hire, and manage AI PMs. Perhaps you're creating an AI pillar in your company. This book will help you get into the mindset of an AI PM and understand the motivations and challenges of the role, as well as the skill sets you should be looking for.

WHAT'S GREAT ABOUT BEING AN AI PM

Just like an architect designs buildings from scratch, being an AI PM means you have a vision of what your product will look like.

You get to set the direction and inspire your team to work together to bring that vision to life. Imagine you've spent months building a product from scratch. Now the work is finished, and users will be able to experience what you've built.

The adrenaline of hitting "launch" and seeing your product come to life is like nothing else.

Also, you will never get bored. As an AI PM, you never stop learning—whether it's about new technologies, large language models (LLMs), or the nuances of mental models. You can't really stay ahead of the curve, because new curves are created all the time.

Most importantly, anyone is welcome in this profession, regardless of their background. There is no formal education or training required to get into AI and product management. AI involves knowledge and skills that you can acquire.

SUBTYPES OF AI PRODUCT MANAGEMENT ROLES

This profession encompasses a wide array of specialized roles, each focused on different aspects of building, scaling, and managing AI-powered products. Depending on the organization, the specific responsibilities of these roles may vary, but the descriptions in the following sections will provide a solid starting point for understanding the diverse roles within the field. Additionally, we'll dive into the concepts of "o-to-1" product management (building new products from the ground up based on an AI technology) versus "1-to-n" product management (enhancing existing products with AI) because this distinction heavily influences the AI Product Development Lifecycle, as you will see in Chapter 2.

There are three main categories of AI product managers: AI builder PMs, AI experiences PMs, and AI-enhanced PMs. *AI builder PMs* focus on developing foundational AI technologies and models, working closely with technical teams to ensure robust system creation. *AI experiences PMs* emphasize crafting engaging and innovative user experiences powered by AI's capabilities. In contrast, *AI-enhanced PMs* leverage AI tools into their own existing workflows, enhancing their productivity. While AI builder PMs and AI experiences PMs often follow a more sequential approach, AI-enhanced PMs span the entire product lifecycle. This book covers all three categories, providing a comprehensive guide to excelling in these dynamic roles (*https://oreil.ly/bN6eo*).

AI experiences PMs concentrate on building AI-driven features that directly enhance user interactions in consumer-facing and enterprise applications. Their work often includes crafting novel features like voice-activated commands in smart home devices, designing AI-generated playlists in music apps, or adding advanced capabilities to wearable tech such as the Oura Ring or Meta's Ray-Ban AI glasses. This role can be more accessible to those without deep technical expertise, as it emphasizes creativity, user empathy, and a high-level understanding of AI's capabilities. Beyond simply knowing how AI works, these PMs excel by weaving AI seamlessly into a cohesive and delightful user journey—balancing automation with user control and ensuring new features truly solve user problems.

Within this category, *ranking PMs* oversee sorting mechanisms for content or products (e.g., search results or social media feeds), grappling with issues like relevance, fairness, and diversity. *Recommendations PMs* build recommendation engines that personalize content, addressing challenges such as the "cold start" problem for new users and the need to prevent content bubbles. *Responsible AI PMs* focus on ethical considerations—ensuring fairness, transparency, and compliance with regulations—while *AI personalization PMs* zero in on individualized user experiences, from personalized learning paths to customized news feeds. An *AI analytics PM* might work on dashboards that use predictive algorithms to deliver actionable insights in real time, whereas a *conversational AI PM* manages chatbots, voice assistants, or other NLP-driven experiences, ensuring smooth, context-aware interactions.

Some real-world job titles in this AI experiences space include:

- Meta: product manager, AI solutions and automation (ASA), GenAI

- Microsoft: product manager, AI

- Anthropic: head of product engineering (not product per se, but engineering manager lead for experiences)

- Intuit: principal product manager, applied AI innovation

- Roblox: senior product manager, creator generative AI and content understanding

To be considered for an AI experiences PM role, it helps to develop a solid awareness of what AI can (and cannot) do, highlighting any domain expertise you already possess. If you come from healthcare and want to lead an AI fitness product, for example, emphasize relevant healthcare insights while demonstrating a well-rounded understanding of AI's limits and ethical implications.

On the other hand, AI builder PMs focus on foundational AI technologies and model-centric work. They often interact closely with researchers and data scientists to develop, train, evaluate, and deploy machine learning models. This function can require more technical depth—especially if you're building or maintaining the entire AI infrastructure. *AI infrastructure/platform PMs* oversee model-training pipelines, data storage solutions, and MLOps tools, ensuring these systems are scalable, performant, and cost-efficient for multiple teams.

Generative AI PMs work with models like GPT-4 or diffusion models to produce text, images, or other media, tackling issues of content quality, efficiency, and ethical use. *Computer vision PMs* manage products that process visual data, from face recognition and AR applications to large-scale image-based searches. *AI security PMs* build or oversee AI solutions aimed at detecting fraud or threats, where real-time response and minimizing false positives/negatives is critical.

Some AI builder PMs operate at the research or "0-to-1" frontier, translating groundbreaking lab discoveries into new commercial products. They set bold visions and guide early-stage, experimental projects—often navigating uncharted territory in AI. If you aspire to a builder role, the best approach is to gain hands-on experience with AI: experiment with open-source models, understand the basics of data pipelines, and learn how to deploy a proof-of-concept. Starting within your current company is often the most direct path, as it lets you build trust with engineering teams while deepening your technical expertise.

Some real-world job titles in this AI experiences space include:

- Roblox: principal product manager, foundation AI

- Scale AI: staff AI product manager, generative AI

- Adobe: principal product manager, generative AI models, Firefly

Finally, AI-enhanced PMs use AI within their own product workflows to be more efficient and data-driven, although their product may not necessarily be AI-centric. They might adopt tools to automate competitive analyses, expedite data exploration, or improve user research—adding an AI "boost" to standard product management tasks throughout the product lifecycle. Chapter 7 expands on recommended AI tools you might want to try out.

Regardless of which category you fall into, the future of product management increasingly involves tapping into AI's potential to deliver unique customer value, create more personalized experiences, and streamline development processes. By learning the right technical basics, staying curious about new AI breakthroughs, and championing an ethical approach to product design, PMs can excel in these fast-evolving roles.

Book Road Map

In the upcoming chapters, we'll walk through the steps of building an AI product from conception to completion. The book will provide frameworks to guide you through the different phases of product development as well as share some of my experiences working with AI products at Meta and Google.

While the product development work is a PM's priority and responsibility, understanding your relationship with different teams working together to bring the product to life, along with the risks and concerns other stakeholders care about, are aspects of the job a PM must not neglect. I want this book to be a road map that guides you through success as you navigate your career in product management. I will share my thoughts and point you to resources and tools that will help you achieve your professional goals. Once we feel comfortable with the responsibilities of an AI PM, we'll switch gears and cover how PMs measure the success of an AI product and how we will mold the AI experience for our end users.

Conclusion

This chapter introduced you to the exciting world of AI product management. It outlined the unique role of an AI PM, where this role fits into enterprises, and why you might want to pursue this field. An AI PM's work is about more than technology; it's about bridging that technology to solve real-world problems for real people.

The AI Product Development Lifecycle

Unlike traditional products, AI-driven products introduce a unique blend of code, data, algorithms, and user experience, creating a distinctive development narrative. The AI Product Development Lifecycle (AIPDL)[1] captures the phases of developing an AI-powered product while ensuring that the product meets users' needs and will find a market fit. In this chapter, I will introduce two types of AI products, 0-to-1 and 1-to-n, and detail how these products are developed following the phases of the AIPDL. Most AI products will follow the AIPDL quite closely, but depending on the product type, the time needed in each phase may vary.

Types of AI Products

The AIPDL depends on the type of AI product you are making. If you work at an early-stage startup, you may work on *0-to-1 products*, applying an emerging technology or model to a new product to create an experience that did not exist before. If you work at a more established organization, you may also work with *1-to-n products*, enhancing, expanding, or adapting an existing product. The AIPDL changes slightly depending on your organization's focus.

The following sections discuss some considerations for managing different AI products.

---

1 This concept is derived from the product development lifecycle (*https://oreil.ly/lnt--*).

0-TO-1 AI PRODUCTS

If you're working on a 0-to-1 product, you might be one of your organization's first AI PMs. This role is ubiquitous in early-stage startups. For example, perhaps you're joining an early-stage self-driving car startup that has just secured funding for its first PM.

The 0-to-1 product type also exists in larger organizations, especially in more research-focused departments with technical expertise in a specific domain. For example, Adobe, Pinterest, and Nextdoor posted AI PM job openings shortly after OpenAI launched ChatGPT. This move acknowledged the transformative potential that LLM technology could bring to their respective platforms, especially considering the vast amounts of data they have. Realizing this potential—and bridging the divide between AI research and solving real-world user problems—requires specialized project management expertise.

In 0-to-1 products, you don't know who the user is or even if there will be one. This means your technology is a blank canvas that you must transform into a solution for a real user problem. The focus of the AIPDL in these cases is not only to develop the product, but also to find a market fit for the novel technology.

1-TO-N AI PRODUCTS

If you're working on a 1-to-n AI product, you are likely looking to scale, enhance, and diversify your organization's established AI product offerings. Companies such as Netflix and Amazon Prime Video are cases in point: leveraging AI to improve video streaming services is an excellent example of a 1-to-n product. It is likely that your goal here is to create personalized user experiences and streamline content delivery. For instance, you might be working to do the following:

- Harness AI to develop a sophisticated recommendation system that learns and adapts according to users' viewing patterns
- Optimize streaming quality dynamically
- Automate the content moderation process

In 1-to-n products, you may have a better understanding of the product–market fit. You can think of 1-to-n products as derivative products or feature upgrades. Just like a 0-to-1 product, the technology required to develop the 1-to-n product will be available, and it is the AI PM's role to introduce the product into the market. For 1-to-n products, the AIPDL focuses on enhancing existing users' experiences and solving pain points.

The AI Product Development Lifecycle

At a high level, the AIPDL is about moving from a business problem to an AI solution that solves that problem. It consists of five stages, depicted in Figure 2-1: ideation, opportunity, developing a concept/prototype, testing and analysis, and rollout (the AI lifecycle is part of the concept/prototype stage). The AIPDL is an iterative process, so each stage might be revisited many times until the product finds its market fit.

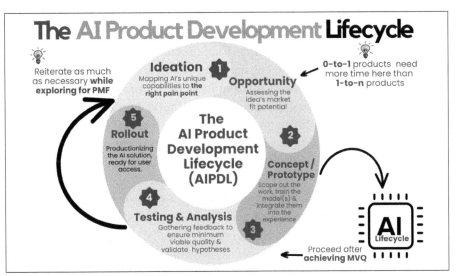

Figure 2-1. The AIPDL (https://oreil.ly/bBNVx) (source: Dr. Marily Nika)

IDEATION

The first stage of the AIPDL is *ideation*. In this stage, you develop your product's initial concept. The goal is to identify the AI features that would benefit your target user segment. The remainder of this section is a step-by-step guide with question prompts to help you and your team steer your creativity in the right direction. You won't always find all the data you need to answer a question, so be prepared to make and test hypotheses and to start again from scratch if you can't validate them.

Step 1: Adopt an innovation-first mindset

Steve Jobs famously said (*https://oreil.ly/361jj*), "People don't know what they want until you show it to them." Not long ago, mobile phones had keyboards and home phone receivers had to be plugged into a wall jack. For mobile phones to have touchscreens was unthinkable, as was the ability to wander around your house while on the phone and not get tangled in long phone cords. So embrace creative thinking, no matter how far-fetched your ideas are. Those ideas could become billion-dollar innovations that revolutionize entire industries.

An AI PM's role isn't just to generate new ideas and recognize opportunities for innovation—places where AI is uniquely positioned to have a significant impact. This requires a mindset of constant innovation and curiosity. You must draw inspiration from various industries, user behaviors, and market gaps. I like to practice creative product ideation by brainstorming how to improve customer–product engagement when using a product. For instance, whenever I order coffee using the Starbucks app, I subconsciously look for aspects of the product that I would improve to enhance user experiences. For example, AI algorithms could predict the busiest times at local storefronts and suggest optimal pickup times to minimize wait times. The Starbucks app could also leverage recommendation algorithms to prioritize displaying frequently purchased items, or even suggest new drinks based on flavor and ingredient preferences. These enhancements can streamline the user experience and make the experience more personalized.

In a 0-to-1 AI product, the aim of the ideation phase is to identify potential use cases in untapped markets and address the pain points of a particular user segment. This requires brainstorming, extensive market research, hypothesizing, and collaboration with AI researchers. Collaboration is critical, as hypotheses are rigorously tested through prototypes and market fit experiments. Each experiment's feedback cycle is geared toward refining the AI solution to fill market gaps and respond to user needs. You might ask questions like "What are the existing user pain points?" and "What are the untapped markets we can reach with new AI innovations?"

For 1-to-n AI products, the emphasis of the ideation phase is on improving what already exists. Working closely with user experience teams and collecting customer feedback is crucial for pinpointing improvement areas. You'll need data insights on current product usage, which can reveal trends and opportunities where AI can enhance value or efficiency. Relevant questions might be "How can AI streamline this feature?" and "How can we use data to improve the user experience?"

Regardless of the product type, ideas should always be user-centric. The ideation stage involves identifying the target user and understanding their use cases, needs, and pain points. Let your customers inspire you to resolve the right problem. Your role is to envision unique ways AI can serve specific users with specific needs. Typically, you want to optimize for market reach and impact. You will need to accurately identify the most significant user segment and determine which problems can be solved in the most feasible and impactful way. Ask yourself: Which user segment should I focus on, and which will be uniquely positioned to benefit from AI's capabilities?

Remember, AI is not a standalone product; it is an ML technology that alone does not add user value. To bring value to current or prospective users, it must be integrated into an experience. Always remember to think about how the technology can enhance a user experience or contribute to solving an unmet need.

Step 2: Understand AI-powered features and their capabilities

AI PMs are the bridge between AI niche technologies and user problems. In the ideation stage, you need to figure out the right problem to solve and how to add value for the users you identify.

Given the unique superpowers AI offers, as discussed in Chapter 1, ask yourself: How can AI uniquely address the specific pain points of that user segment, making their experience more efficient, enjoyable, or valuable? In 1-to-n products, you already have some user insights that can guide you to enhance your current offerings. For 0-to-1 products, you will need to be creative about how to create an experience that finds product–market fit. Table 2-1 maps the kinds of user experiences that AI and GenAI's superpowers can enable.

Table 2-1. What AI and GenAI's superpowers can enable for users

Superpower	What it enables for users	Example
Learning from data	Real-time insights and suggestions based on user-generated content and historical data	• Whoop (*https://www.whoop.com/us/en*) (wearable fitness tracker that provides predictive insights about recovery, sleep, and strain) • Fitbod (*https://fitbod.me*) (strength training app that predicts the optimal workout based on past performance and fatigue levels)
Personalization at scale	Tailored recommendations and experiences that continuously adapt to user preferences, behaviors, and moods	Spotify's AI DJ feature (*https://oreil.ly/75sUe*)

Superpower	What it enables for users	Example
Generating new content	Ability to create custom text, images, audio, and video at scale	• Google Gemini (*https://oreil.ly/_G3pp*) • Claude (*https://claude.ai*) • ChatGPT (*https://chatgpt.com*)
Distillation and summarization	Simplifies complex information into digestible insights or summaries, making content easier to consume and understand, and supporting knowledge discovery and decision augmentation	• NotebookLM (*https://notebooklm.google*) • Otter.ai (*http://otter.ai*) • Tableau (*https://www.tableau.com*) with AI-powered analytics • IBM Watson (*https://oreil.ly/ZA4AM*) (used for healthcare decisions)
Prediction and forecasting	Predictive analytics that forecast trends and generate actionable insights for better decision making	Kensho (*https://kensho.com*) (S&P Global's AI-powered predictive insights for financial markets)
Real-time adaptation	Instant, dynamic responses in conversational interactions and content generation that evolves with the user's needs	Duolingo (*https://www.duolingo.com*) (language learning app that adjusts lessons based on user performance)
Automating workflows	Smarter automation that optimizes tasks based on real-time data and contextual factors, enhancing efficiency	Zaps by Zapier (*https://oreil.ly/Pe76v*)
Creative collaboration	Assists users in brainstorming, generating ideas, and refining creative projects such as music, writing, or art	Adobe Firefly (*https://oreil.ly/F4T-4*) (AI tools for creative workflows)
Immersive and interactive spaces	Dynamic, interactive environments that adapt to user input, offering more engaging and personalized virtual experiences	• Rec Room (*https://recroom.com*) • Roblox (*https://www.roblox.com*)

Superpower	What it enables for users	Example
Error detection and mitigation	Identifies errors or inefficiencies in processes or content, ensuring higher accuracy and performance	Grammarly (*https://www.grammarly.com*) (real-time grammar and tone correction)
Reasoning and intent understanding	Accurately interprets the user's intentions, even when expressed in vague, ambiguous, or incomplete terms, ensuring better alignment with the user's needs	Gemini, ChatGPT, and Claude, which use advanced reasoning to deduce the true meaning behind user inputs
Multimodality	Allows seamless integration and processing of multiple input types, such as text, audio, images, and video, enabling more versatile and intuitive interactions	Gemini 2.0, DALL-E, and Whisper, which accept and process various forms of input and combinations of input for tasks such as generating text from images, or transcribing audio to text or real-time voice responses
Humanlike conversation	Facilitates natural and engaging interactions that mimic human conversation, fostering deeper connections and improving user satisfaction	Conversational agents (especially with audio-out) that simulate humanlike dialogue

A single user's product experience can utilize multiple AI superpowers. For example, in healthcare applications, personalization at scale, prediction and forecasting, and the ability to reinvent product interactions are AI superpowers that can transform how individuals seek medical care.

With a highly accurate predictive model, you might deploy AI algorithms to aid doctors in patient diagnosis, treatment recommendations, and drug discovery. For areas with little access to healthcare, you can deploy these models to increase the availability of care to individuals in need.

Step 3: Brainstorm with your team

The ideation phase in AI product development is where the seeds of innovation are planted. It's the perfect time to kick off a product requirements document (PRD), where you'll begin framing the problem and jotting down potential AI-powered feature ideas. After outlining initial concepts in the PRD, collaborative brainstorming with your team becomes critical. This is where you start turning vague ideas into feasible AI solutions. You can find a sample PRD structure in the Appendix.

AI product development, in particular, benefits immensely from diverse perspectives during brainstorming. Your team members may have different insights into data sources, model capabilities, user needs, and ethical considerations. By bringing these viewpoints together, you can refine initial ideas, challenge assumptions, and explore AI solutions that you might not have considered on your own. Conversations about feasibility—such as the data needed for model training or the potential impact of AI on user experience—are crucial to setting realistic goals for the product team and aligning on what's possible within the current state of AI technology.

Your team is your best source of talent and inspiration. They know your domain, understand the unique challenges of integrating AI, and likely are eager to contribute innovative ideas. If you have a large team, select four or five core members with diverse skills, such as data science, UX design, ethics, and domain expertise, and tag them in the PRD or invite them to the brainstorming session. Diversity in thought leads to more creative and comprehensive AI solutions, ensuring that you consider all aspects, from data acquisition to model deployment.

If you plan to have an actual meeting, promote a creative and focused environment. Consider blocking off three to four hours for an in-depth brainstorming session. AI ideas often require time to explore possibilities, weigh trade-offs, and discuss data requirements, so giving your team ample time to warm up and dive deep is essential. Encourage participants to limit nonbrainstorming activities; mute notifications, pause emails, and keep side conversations off the table to maintain focus.

Before the creative exploration begins, remind the team of the specific AI-focused goal. Encourage your collaborators from other product areas (e.g., development, sales, ethics, R&D) to identify existing product gaps that they interface with that AI can uniquely fill. From those gaps, ideate on solutions that leverage AI's capabilities to address user needs. Setting clear goals will help guide the discussion and keep it centered on exploring AI's potential impact.

To help the team align on AI goals and prospects, start the session with a small reflection exercise that asks everyone to list their current projects, aspirational projects, and moonshot ideas:

Current projects
> This helps identify areas where AI might enhance or automate existing features. Use this time to communicate and brainstorm with different teams on how AI will add value to the product, such as using ML to optimize an ongoing process.

Aspirational projects
> These are products the team wishes they had time to work on. This exercise can uncover interest in AI-related trends, such as personalization or intelligent automation, that may be worth exploring further in your product strategy.

Moonshot ideas
> Encourage the team to think about ambitious, resource-unconstrained AI products. What if data limitations and model complexity were no object? These blue-sky ideas can inspire innovative AI applications that push the boundaries of what your product can achieve.

After creating the lists, instruct team members to select the top 10% of ideas that offer the most value to key user segments. Prioritizing the high-value customers ensures that the team focuses on impactful projects. Once the lists are ready, have people share their ideas with the group. Throughout the discussion, remember to identify recurring themes and interests to pinpoint the most promising projects that align with team strengths and organizational goals.

Here are some key dos and don'ts that I strongly recommend when brainstorming ideas for your product:

- Dos:

  — Do solve the right problem.

    Every great product idea starts with an important problem, but is it the right one to leverage AI? You must validate whether users are bothered enough by that problem before jumping into solutions. Identifying product gaps, or pain points users continue to experience, can lead to building revolutionary products. Take Dyson, for example. This company recognized that people disliked having to plug in a cord to vacuum and thus designed the first cordless vacuum, the Dyson DC01. Now Dyson is a market leader in the industry.

  — Do understand the impact of each feature.

    You can launch a new feature for your already launched product. Before doing so, consider how this new feature will impact your existing features. Each new feature should either improve or not interfere with your previous features or the overall product mission. In AI, this is more important than ever, as strategy plays a key role in staying ahead in this fast-paced environment.

- Don'ts:

  — Don't fall into the "shiny AI object" trap.

    Don't launch products just because the technology behind them is "cool." Do your homework: make sure your product road map aligns with your business objectives for your product to succeed.

  — Don't talk about a "hunch."

    A great PM has great estimation and analytical skills. Back your "hunches" with data: Have others done something similar? If so, what was the return on investment? With data to support your ideas, you'll be more likely to get buy-in on your proposal.

Step 4: Know your customers by using the RICE framework

If you're developing a 0-to-1 AI product, the final ideation step is crucial: you must study the needs of your target customers thoroughly. The most effective source of insight and inspiration comes from actively listening to your users. Pay close attention to their feedback, the shortcomings they point out, and the difficulties they face. Feedback can be found anywhere. Customer service interactions are a great place to start because these interactions are often much more personal. Online reviews are another good option for quality feedback; social media is a great place to get lots of input.

Remember to carefully filter for quality when pulling feedback from social media platforms. How you do so may depend on the type of feedback you are looking for. For example, a comment saying "bad product" is not meaningful. Instead, you may want to perform a targeted search for reasons why users are frustrated with the product; for example, "I don't like the movie recommendations I get." Analyze whether AI can uniquely address these issues. For instance, if users express frustration with the recommendation algorithm, you can implement AI solutions to offer better personalization and immediate support to minimize user frustrations. By identifying and understanding these specific pain points, you can determine how AI might offer a distinct solution to resolve existing problems and enhance your users' experience. By this stage in the AI product development process, you likely have a good understanding of the user segment you're targeting and a long list of potential AI-powered features. However, not all features can be pursued at once, so prioritization is crucial. This is where frameworks come into play, providing structure to help you make informed decisions about which features to focus on.

I recommend using the RICE framework (*https://oreil.ly/JfqjN*) for feature prioritization. This framework helps you objectively evaluate each feature based on four key factors: reach, impact, confidence, and effort. By scoring your ideas across these dimensions, you can identify the features that will deliver the most value with the least amount of resources:

Reach
> Estimate how many users the feature will affect within a given time frame. For example, if you're building a recommendation feature for a video streaming service, consider the number of binge-watchers who will engage with this new functionality in a month.

Impact

> Measure the potential impact of the feature on your key metrics, such as user engagement or retention. Use a scale (e.g., 3 for high impact, 2 for medium, 1 for low) to quantify this.

Confidence

> Assess how confident you are in your estimates for reach and impact. If you have strong data or user research backing your predictions, your confidence should be high. Confidence is crucial in AI product development because sometimes the data or algorithm feasibility may not be entirely clear at the ideation phase. Use percentages to reflect this (e.g., 80% confident).

Effort

> Estimate the total amount of work required to implement the feature, typically measured in person-months. Consider both the technical complexity (e.g., data collection, model training, and integration) and any nontechnical efforts (e.g., design and user testing).

The RICE score for each feature is calculated using the formula shown in Figure 2-2.

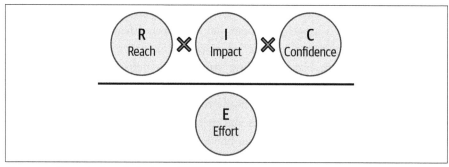

Figure 2-2. Formula for calculating a RICE score

A higher RICE score indicates a feature that will deliver more value for less effort, making it a strong candidate for implementation. Let's say you want to build a feature specifically for binge-watchers on your video streaming platform, with the goal of increasing watch time. You have three potential feature ideas to evaluate:

Personalized binge-watching recommendations
Using AI to provide hyper-personalized content suggestions based on binge-watching habits.

"Continue watching" smart notifications
AI-driven notifications that remind users to pick up where they left off in a series at the right time of the week or day, based on the user's prior history and calendar.

Enhanced watchlist management
When a user presses a button to express interest in specific shows, all of which will be grouped together in a *watchlist*. An AI-powered watchlist would prioritize these shows based on the user's preferences and watching history.

Table 2-2 shows how you might use the RICE framework to prioritize these features.

Table 2-2. Prioritizing features using RICE scores

Feature	Reach	Impact	Confidence	Effort	RICE score
Personalized binge-watching recommendations	8,000	3	90%	4	5,400
"Continue watching" smart notifications	6,000	2	80%	2	4,800
Enhanced watchlist management	5,000	2	70%	3	2,333

In this example, "Personalized binge-watching recommendations" has the highest RICE score, indicating that it offers the most value relative to the effort required. This feature would likely be the best one to pursue first if your goal is to maximize watch time for binge-watchers.

Note

You might consider introducing an additional parameter alongside effort, called "AI investment." This parameter would represent the complexity involved in training or integrating a model into an experience, factoring in aspects such as data collection, resource allocation, and hardware/cost requirements to achieve the desired quality. This would transform the RICE model into R × I × C / E × A (*https://oreil.ly/RZ37S*).

OPPORTUNITY

Once you have a clear idea of the AI feature(s) that would benefit your target user segment the most, the next phase involves assessing the idea's potential market fit. It's good to start this phase with a hypothesis in mind. A o-to-1 product opportunity example would be:

> Binge watchers are more likely to keep returning to our streaming platform if their recommendations for what to watch next are accurate.

A 1-to-n product opportunity example would be:

> Busy professionals' fitness will improve if they use a discreet wearable step-tracking device that provides meaningful insights and recommendations about their daily lifestyle.

During the opportunity phase, it is time to assess whether to move forward with your hypothesis. Is there a good signal that you will find a product–market fit with a solution for that specific user segment? During this phase, the goal is to understand how big the opportunity is by diving deep into competitor products, alternative solutions, market size, and timing for a solution like yours. A thorough market analysis is vital to a strong product value proposition, as it will help you avoid wasting resources (money, effort, time) on a nonviable idea.

Your goal as an AI PM is to find product–market fit by ensuring that your idea is feasible from a technical perspective, desirable to users, and viable from a business perspective.

Product–market fit

Product–market fit refers to whether a feature meets the needs and solves the pain points of a specific market segment.

Achieving product–market fit is crucial for the success of AI ventures, as it demonstrates that the AI solution works technically and is valuable and relevant to its users. This concept is widely discussed in business and technology literature, including in the work of Marc Andreessen, who popularized the term in the context of startups and technology products. While Andreessen's discussions were not AI specific, his principles apply to the field of AI, given the importance of developing technologies that align with market needs.

For more in-depth exploration and examples of product–market fit in AI, excellent resources include Andreessen's writings and the Lean startup methodology proposed by Eric Ries,[2] which emphasizes rapid prototyping and user feedback. Many AI startups and projects have adopted these principles to ensure that their innovations not only are technologically advanced but also meet the real-world demands of users.

Product–market fit is achieved when the product meets three criteria (see Figure 2-3):

Business viability
> The product can generate sustainable revenue in a competitive marketplace. Business viability means having a capturable market space, a profitable revenue model, and a healthy and responsive economic environment. To assess a product's business viability, you must evaluate risk, calculate the return on investment (ROI), and ensure regulatory compliance.

Technical feasibility
> Your organization has the resources (technical experts, hardware, software, data, computing power, etc.) to support the envisioned features and functionality. Identifying the necessary technical resources for the project helps set realistic expectations and goals, ultimately minimizing go-to-market risks.

User desirability
> The product effectively solves the target market's pain points.

All three criteria must be met, or it isn't a product–market fit, as you can see from the diagram in Figure 2-3.

Let's take a closer look at the criteria for product–market fit.

---

2 Marc Andreessen, "The Only Thing That Matters," June 25, 2007; Eric Ries, *The Lean Startup: How Today's Entrepreneurs Use Continuous Innovation to Create Radically Successful Businesses* (Crown Business, 2011).

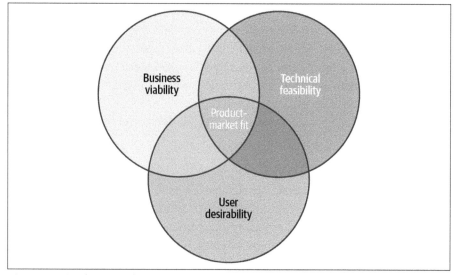

Figure 2-3. Visualizing product–market fit

Business viability

Business viability involves comprehensive go-to-market strategies, customer acquisition, and retention tactics. Achieving business viability confirms that the product can sustain itself in the market, attract investment, and grow over time. To predict business viability, you will need to conduct in-depth research to understand where the market lacks solutions and how an AI product could fill that void.

This research often starts with understanding your target market and the problem your product solves. This requires thorough market research to identify gaps in existing solutions and validate the demand for your product. Tools such as surveys, focus groups, and user interviews can uncover customer pain points and expectations. In larger tech companies, you will probably have an in-house UX researcher who will partner with you to craft the right questions for the users. Smaller companies and startups often outsource this work to external agencies (such as Upwork) or use websites that connect them directly to users to answer questions. Questions reach users through surveys, focus groups, online one-on-one interviews, or simply in-app feedback. You can also use AI tools for market research, such as Komo (*https://komo.ai*) and You.com (*https://you.com*).

In addition to knowing your end user, paying attention to your competitors helps you uniquely position your product, ensuring that it delivers a clear advantage over alternatives. Learn and get inspired by the competition. Chances are good that more organizations are operating in similar domains to yours. It is important to familiarize yourself with their offerings and solutions and to follow their blogs, research publications, and other communication channels.

ROI analysis. Calculating a project's ROI requires a thorough analysis of the initial costs and the anticipated benefits. ROI is derived from the net profit from an investment divided by the total investment cost, as shown in Figure 2-4. The calculation must encompass *all* direct expenses related to AI integration, such as software development and acquisition costs, as well as indirect expenses, such as training and potential productivity losses (e.g., staff turnover or sick leaves) during implementation. The net returns should include a quantified value of the expected gains from AI integration, such as improved efficiency, enhanced product features, increased sales, and potential marketshare expansion.

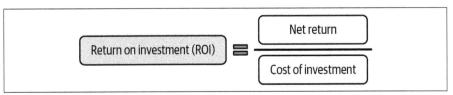

Figure 2-4. ROI formula

There are a handful of strategies you can use to maximize ROI for an AI project. First, integrating AI should align closely with the company's strategic goals. Target areas where AI can deliver significant improvements or address key challenges. Second, ensuring the quality and availability of data is crucial, since any AI model's effectiveness heavily depends on the data it is trained on. Investing in proprietary systems and internal data-collection practices can dramatically enhance the outcomes of AI initiatives. A third strategy is to account for scalability and flexibility to accommodate future growth. Incorporating scalability early in the design process will increase long-term ROI by minimizing the costs of maintenance and upgrades.

Ensuring the adoption and continuous optimization of new releases or updates is vital for any product to realize its full ROI. Secure end users' buy-in by offering customer support and feedback loops. This contributes to building strong and persistent customer engagement with the product.

By executing and maintaining AI integration strategies such as these, PMs can significantly enhance the value of AI investments.

Monetizing AI features. Monetizing AI features introduces unique opportunities and challenges that can significantly influence product–market fit and business viability. Companies typically adopt either direct or indirect monetization strategies (*https://oreil.ly/5zhTn*), each suited to different contexts.

Direct monetization strategies might involve charging separately for the AI feature as an add-on, bundling it with a price increase, or offering it as a standalone product. This approach works well when customers recognize clear added value or when AI features entail high operational costs, such as compute and storage. Alternatively, *indirect monetization strategies* integrate AI features into existing packages without altering prices, leveraging them to enhance adoption, retention, or usage of core products. This can be particularly effective for companies seeking to refine their AI capabilities before attaching a price tag. The choice of strategy should align with the target audience's willingness to pay and the strategic goals of driving user adoption versus maximizing immediate ROI.

Risk evaluation. It's crucial to evaluate the risks associated with developing a novel AI product. These risks span technological, market, and financial aspects. Managing *technological risks* involves assessing the maturity of your AI technologies and sourcing, utilizing, and protecting quality data. Handling *market risks* involves understanding the hurdles to user adoption, analyzing the competitive landscape, and navigating a changing regulatory scene. Dealing with *financial risks* involves managing the cost overruns inherent in AI development, projecting revenue accurately, and ensuring sufficient funding to sustain the development phase until market launch.

Equally important is identifying the best time to introduce a specific AI solution. Your chances of success are greatly diminished if the market is not ready for a novel product. Factors such as market readiness, the state of technological infrastructure among potential users, and current demand play a pivotal role in finding product–market fit. Broader socioeconomic blockers, such as economic downturns, regulatory shifts, or societal resistance to AI technologies, can also significantly impact the feasibility and timing of launching a new AI product.

Assessing these elements helps you identify current opportunities and potential challenges that could affect the product's success. Finding the right go-to-market time is about achieving a tricky balance between these risk assessment pillars. Evaluating the risks and timing considerations allows companies to make informed decisions, increasing the product's potential for success in the market.

Regulatory compliance. For nascent technology industries such as AI initiatives, business viability also entails weighing the regulatory, ethical, and social implications of deploying AI solutions. Understanding and ensuring compliance with industry regulations and standards is a complex yet critical process for new technologies, especially during market scoping and development. There are many eyes on AI products due to increased scrutiny of their potential impact on privacy, security, and ethical considerations.

Depending on where and with whom they do business, companies must navigate a patchwork of regional and sector-specific regulations, such as the GDPR (*https://gdpr-info.eu*) in the United Kingdom, the Artificial Intelligence Act (EU AI Act) (*https://oreil.ly/2Onuo*) in the European Union, and the Health Insurance Portability and Accountability Act (HIPAA) (*https://oreil.ly/-B6vg*) in the United States. Complying with these laws involves conducting comprehensive audits of AI systems to ensure that they meet legal requirements for data handling, user consent, transparency, and accountability. Adhering to principles of transparency and accountability often requires AI solutions to deploy explainable AI (XAI) (*https://oreil.ly/xO2y_*) practices, which make AI decisions understandable to end users and regulators. XAI frequently enlists open source tools, such as SHAP (*https://oreil.ly/2G9Gm*), LIME (*https://oreil.ly/IIVky*), and InterpretML (*https://interpret.ml*)) ,to explain to end users how the model works, its potential biases, and its outputs. There is a huge community of researchers exploring the value of XAI practices, and numerous books cover methods for making ML more explainable.

As AI technologies and the regulatory landscape evolve, maintaining compliance will mean establishing processes for regularly reviewing and adjusting your AI systems. For instance, new laws may require updates to your privacy policies, data processing agreements, and user consent mechanisms. Stay informed about emerging guidelines and frameworks that influence public expectations and regulatory developments. Above all, as an AI PM, you must engage with legal technology and with data-law experts and compliance officers to help navigate these complexities and ensure that product updates are legally sound.

Many companies are realizing the priceless value of customer trust. Trust is a critical asset in the digital age, especially for AI-driven products, where concerns about data privacy, security, and ethical use are paramount. To be a successful AI PM, you must position your products as a trustworthy solution to users' problems. Ensuring legal compliance and ethical integrity in your products mitigates the risk of financial penalties and legal implications, while building a strong foundation for AI sustainability and humanitarian use of data builds trust with users and stakeholders.

Technical feasibility

Conducting a thorough technical feasibility assessment is imperative for developing an AI-driven product. The process begins with sharing the envisioned AI functionalities with technical teams, engineers, and scientists to gather preliminary feedback. The teams should focus on whether the existing technological infrastructure can support developing the proposed features. This is less about detailing specifics and more about understanding potential technical constraints and opportunities.

The availability of the data required to train and build the AI model is at the core of technical feasibility. Collaborating closely with technical teams helps identify the type, quality, and quantity of data needed. This step is crucial, as data availability and quality directly influence the practicality of developing AI features as well as their adoption success. It's a phase where theoretical concepts confront the realities of data constraints and guide your adjustments to the project's scope and direction.

User desirability

Determining whether users are willing to pay to solve a particular pain point is central to validating a product's commercial viability. This process involves a mix of market research, experimentation, and direct engagement with potential users. Here's how you can approach getting to the answer and know when you've come close.

Start with your due diligence. Look into existing solutions and how those solutions are priced. Look at the competitive landscape to give yourself a benchmark valuation for the problem you are trying to solve. Study competing value propositions to identify gaps or opportunities for differentiation. Once you've found a position in the market to fill, conduct surveys and interviews with your target audience to gauge market interest in a new solution and their willingness to pay. The survey can include questions such as "How often does [pain point] impact your daily life?" and "What do you do to minimize [pain point]?"

Your questions should be designed not just to uncover a yes or no answer, but also to explore the depth of the pain point, how it affects users, and the value they would place on solving it. Additionally, techniques such as the Van Westendorp Pricing Model (*https://oreil.ly/NDd5K*) can be useful in approaching the question of a fair price.

Having a prototype or a minimum viable product (MVP) is a great way to engage customers with the product and observe the direct value end users obtain. An MVP is the first iteration of the product. It has the basic features for early customers to use and later provides the product team with feedback for future improvements. MVPs have many uses. Not only are they a great starting point to put in front of end users, but they are also a great tool to help product managers test their pricing strategy. Experimentation methods such as A/B testing can be particularly effective here. As a PM, you can experiment with different pricing tiers and strategies to see which one yields better conversion rates or customer satisfaction. Take note of feedback about the product and its perceived value at different price points. Customer sentiment will affect brand awareness and brand image.

Knowing when you have reached the answer comes down to analyzing the survey and experimental data. Look for patterns in how users respond to pricing questions on the survey and compare that with their actual behavior during MVP testing. If there is a consistent willingness to pay and that price range aligns with your cost structures and profit margins, you've found a sweet spot.

Even if the stars align, it's important to continue monitoring and testing as you scale, as market conditions and consumer perceptions are prone to change.

I find the scale in Figure 2-5 to be very useful in assessing whether you have enough data points to know if you are close to product–market fit. If the signals increasingly come from farther to the right, you are nearing product–market fit. If the signals increasingly come from farther to the left, you are moving away from product–market fit.

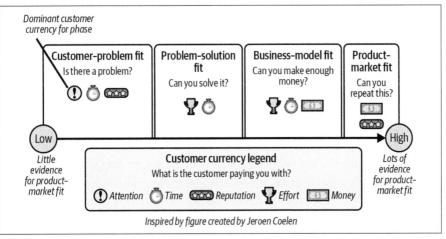

Figure 2-5. Product–market fit scale

Achieving AI product–market fit

To holistically gauge product–market fit, it's essential to revisit the three foundational pillars that define it: business viability, technical feasibility, and user desirability. Together, these pillars provide a holistic view of the opportunity phase, ensuring that your product isn't just innovative or technically achievable, but also something users will want and the market can sustain. It's important to emphasize that achieving product–market fit requires meeting all three of these criteria. If one pillar is weak or missing, the product is unlikely to succeed.

To push this point further, imagine you are developing an AI music suggestion algorithm that recommends music based on mood. This AI would analyze your emotions based on content engagement, audio capture, and biosignal data to recommend music that matches your mood. I can see users being interested in having an AI-generated playlist that captures nuances in emotion and atmosphere. This music recommendation algorithm can be achieved with existing ML networks. What may lead to poor AI product–market fit is low business viability.

This AI product may face privacy and social monitoring concerns. Additionally, gathering sensitive emotional data from biometric data raises significant ethical and legal issues. While there may be interest in the product and the cost to build it is low, the various business risks and uncertainties in regulation will hinder its success. Finding product–market fit is a challenging balance and will require careful product design to bring the market something people are excited about.

CONCEPT AND PROTOTYPE

When you've moved past the ideation and initial validation phases, it's time to focus on building the MVP for your AI product. An AI MVP is more than just a basic version of a product. It's a strategic build designed to demonstrate AI's potential within the targeted use case. As Eric Ries famously said, "The minimum viable product is that version of a new product which allows a team to collect the maximum amount of validated learning about customers with the least effort."[3] For AI products, this means creating a version that not only showcases immediate value but also hints at future capabilities.

It's important to distinguish an AI MVP from a prototype. A prototype is typically an early experimental model used to explore feasibility, illustrate how the AI could function, and test different ideas in a controlled environment. While

---

3 Eric Ries, *What Is an MVP?* (Lean Startup Co., 2009).

prototypes are valuable for concept exploration, they don't necessarily provide real, usable value to the end user—they're more about showing what *could* be possible.

An AI MVP, in contrast, is a functional product designed to add value from day one. Unlike a prototype, which might simulate experiences with preset interactions or mock data, an AI MVP integrates with real-world systems, interacts with live data, and delivers tangible solutions to user problems. This shift from simulation to actual user engagement is what makes the AI MVP a critical step in the product development lifecycle.

Building an AI MVP comes with its own set of challenges and considerations that set it apart from traditional MVPs. One critical component of building the AI MVP is the *model training*, which can be seen as a mini-lifecycle within this stage. This involves selecting the appropriate algorithms, gathering relevant data, training the model, and iterating based on initial performance. It's an iterative process that enables the AI to learn and improve, forming the core of how your MVP operates. We'll dive into more detail about this process and the entire AI lifecycle in Chapter 3, where you'll get a comprehensive overview of the technical concepts that underpin each stage.

Unlike a typical MVP, which might focus solely on building the simplest version of a product, an AI MVP needs to do four things: require putting together a hardcoded experience, demonstrate integration compatibility, showcase domain-specific expertise, and add value from day one. Let's take a look at each of these.

Require putting together a hardcoded experience

When building an AI MVP, it's sometimes necessary to hardcode certain aspects of the product to demonstrate its potential without investing excessive time in developing a fully automated system. This approach allows you to quickly validate your concept and showcase key functionalities, even if the underlying AI models aren't fully optimized or trained yet.

In many cases, AI MVPs involve combining different models or techniques to create a hybrid solution. However, building all aspects of the system from scratch can be time-consuming and resource intensive. This is where hardcoding comes in. For example, if you're developing a recommendation engine but don't yet have enough data to train a personalized model, you might hardcode certain rules to simulate how the recommendations would work. Similarly, in a chatbot MVP, you might include predefined responses for common queries while the more advanced NLP capabilities are still being refined.

By hardcoding specific elements, you can avoid wasting time on aspects of the product that don't need to be fully automated at this stage. This approach helps keep the MVP focused on demonstrating the AI's core value proposition, allowing stakeholders to experience its potential while you continue to develop and iterate the more complex AI-driven components in parallel.

Demonstrate (ideally low-effort) integration compatibility

For AI products to be valuable, they need to integrate seamlessly with potential existing systems, typically through an API. Organizations (especially larger ones) usually operate within complex software ecosystems, so it's important for the MVP to showcase its ability to fit into these workflows. This not only proves the technical feasibility of the product, but also shows stakeholders that it can enhance existing processes rather than disrupt them.

When designing your AI MVP, think about how it will connect with the other tools and systems in the organization. For example, if you're building a predictive analytics tool for sales forecasting, the MVP should be able to pull data from existing customer relationship management (CRM) systems and export its insights to other platforms. Including a basic API or integration layer in the MVP can go a long way in demonstrating its potential to scale and adapt within the company's current ecosystem. Even simple, sample integrations can be powerful proof points during presentations and validation phases.

Showcase domain-specific expertise

One of the critical success factors for an AI product is its ability to understand the specific domain in which it operates. For an MVP, it's crucial to exhibit this domain knowledge early on. Whether the focus is on medical diagnostics, retail customer segmentation, or financial analytics, showing that the AI can handle domain-specific nuances will be key to gaining stakeholder trust.

This often means training the model using a small but high-quality dataset specific to your domain. For example, if you're building an AI diagnostic tool for healthcare, you might use a set of anonymized medical images to illustrate the model's capability to identify a particular condition. The goal is not to cover every possible use case at this stage, but to demonstrate that the AI is capable of producing accurate, relevant results that fit into the real-world scenarios of your target vertical.

Add value from day one

AI MVPs are different from traditional software MVPs in that they need to add immediate value to demonstrate their potential. While AI applications are designed to improve over time with additional data, your MVP still has to deliver tangible benefits right from the start. This could take the form of a more personalized user experience, operational efficiency gains, or actionable insights derived from existing data.

When designing the MVP, focus on features that can provide clear, immediate benefits. For instance, an AI-powered recommendation system for an ecommerce platform should at least offer some relevant product suggestions to users based on basic input data. It doesn't need to be perfect, but it should validate the concept and hint at how the AI can grow more effective over time as it collects and learns from user interactions.

Building a feedback loop into the MVP is a simple way to illustrate how the product can learn and improve. For example, including a mechanism that collects data on user interactions—such as which product recommendations are clicked on—can provide valuable insights that can be used to fine-tune the model in future iterations. This also allows you to demonstrate the AI's capacity for growth and adaptation, even at this early stage.

TESTING AND ANALYSIS

The testing and analysis phase is a crucial stage in developing any AI-driven product, serving as a bridge between prototype development and market launch. During this phase, the product, now in near-final form, undergoes rigorous evaluation to assess its performance, user acceptance, and market viability.

This process starts with structured feedback sessions involving users who closely match the target personas defined earlier in the development process. Like the earlier feedback sessions, these are designed to gather in-depth insights into how the product addresses the identified pain points, its ease of use, and overall satisfaction. This phase often consists of a beta or phased release to a cohort of selected customers. For example, in the gaming industry, new updates or patches to a game may have a beta release to a set of game testers, who then provide feedback on the gameplay before mass release. This feedback is instrumental in validating your initial hypotheses about the product's value proposition and identifying any gaps or areas for improvement.

Feedback collection can take various forms, including surveys, interviews, focus groups, and simulations. Each form provides unique insights into the product's impact and usability. Advanced analytics and AI tools can also contribute to this phase by scanning user interactions for patterns that indicate satisfaction, engagement, and potential friction points. This stage is about gathering a comprehensive understanding of the user experience, which informs your decisions on whether the product meets the needs and expectations set out at the concept stage.

The culmination of the testing and analysis phase is the critical *Go/No-Go Decision*. This pivotal moment requires stakeholders to assess the gathered data and feedback to determine the product's readiness for the market. Several factors weigh into this decision, including the product's technical readiness, user satisfaction, market conditions, and competitor landscape. The Go/No-Go Decision is not just about whether the product works as intended, but whether it's poised for adoption and success in the competitive market.

If the decision is a "Go," the product moves toward launch with confidence in its market fit and potential for success. If it's a "No-Go," this doesn't necessarily mean abandonment, but rather, a return to the drawing board. This could consist of revisiting the opportunity phase to address specific issues identified during testing, or reevaluating the market strategy. This phase underscores the iterative nature of product development and the importance of experimentation and data-driven analysis when carving out a niche in the market.

ROLLOUT

The rollout or deployment phase marks a significant milestone in the AIPDL, transitioning from development and testing to making the product available to the target market. This phase is not the culmination of the product journey, but the beginning of its real-world application and continuous evolution. As such, meticulous planning and execution are required to ensure a smooth launch, followed by ongoing maintenance and improvement efforts to sustain the product's market relevance. Let's start with the launch and what PMs should look out for.

A successful product launch hinges on a meticulously crafted marketing and promotion strategy alongside a robust logistics and supply chain management plan. The marketing plan should define clear target user segments, communicate strong messaging, and select the optimal channels to promote the product, such as television, print, and social media. Generating excitement is also an effective tactic. Releasing previews and offering early access is a great way to create a buzz and build anticipation.

In my experience, the most effective marketing strategies will build synergies between the different promotional activities and synchronize events along a predetermined timeline. Concurrently, ensuring a reliable, resilient supply chain and logistics system is critical for physical products. This means allocating sufficient inventory levels and scheduling shipping arrangements, thereby ensuring readiness to meet demand efficiently at launch.

The launch phase demands seamless execution, requiring all hands on deck to ensure that every facet of the launch plan unfolds according to the established timeline. This phase is characterized by high coordination and readiness, vigilant monitoring of real-time feedback, and maintaining the momentum of a positive launch experience. Perfectly executing these plans sets a strong foundation for the product's success.

Upon deployment, the focus shifts to monitoring and maintaining the product system. In addition to regularly evaluating the accuracy and performance of the AI models, the post-deployment team must schedule maintenance checks to ensure that the AI features are operating as intended. This often means continuously providing the AI system with new data to adapt and learn from. As models continue to update and retrain on new data, practicing vigilance against potential biases and ethical issues is paramount. Implementing checks for fairness and bias detection not only upholds regulatory requirements but also bolsters user trust in our products.

The phases in the AIPDL are iterative and cyclical, and the rollout phase is no different. Post-deployment teams will continue to monitor market trends and regulatory changes and then implement updates to the product. This iterative approach allows for fine-tuning of features, improving user experiences, and adding new functionalities to meet emerging needs and preferences. By continuing to enhance the features, you will ensure that the product will remain competitive amid the rapidly evolving technology landscape. The rollout phase is not merely about delivering the product to the market, but about setting the foundation for sustained growth.

Conclusion

This chapter conceptualized the five stages of the AIPDL: ideation, opportunity, concept and prototype, testing and analysis, and rollout. Now you are equipped with the overarching strategies and decisions involved with the creation of a product, from a seed in someone's brain to the finalized product used by millions of people.

The product development lifecycle encapsulates the transformative journey of turning innovative ideas into market-ready products. The process emphasizes the importance of meticulous planning, continuous feedback, and iterative improvement. As the product moves from concept to creation, collaboration among designers, engineers, and developers is crucial for overcoming technical challenges.

As a PM, developing a novel product is rewarding and exciting, but it's most certainly not something done by just one person. In Chapter 3, we will take a look at the skills you'll need to become a successful product manager.

3

Essential AI
PM Knowledge

In Chapter 2, we mapped the AI PM's role to each phase of the AIPDL. Unlike their counterparts in traditional product management, AI PMs must carefully navigate advancing AI technologies in ever-changing market demands. Marrying unique product value propositions with a precise market fit gives products a competitive edge and propels industries toward groundbreaking innovations. As businesses increasingly use AI to drive decision making, optimize operations, and personalize customer interactions, the demand for skilled AI PMs has surged. These professionals are at the forefront, developing innovative products to solve unmet needs.

In this chapter, we explore the essential skills that product managers need to transition into roles focused on AI. Moving from traditional to AI product management can be done without starting from scratch. Many core skills you have honed—such as project oversight, stakeholder communication, and strategic thinking—serve as a solid foundation in this new arena. However, AI product management also demands specialized capabilities.

AI PMs must possess technical understanding and strategic foresight to navigate the unique challenges of AI products. As an AI PM, you will be more than a project overseer; you will be the visionary who can discern and balance human needs with machine possibilities. This role requires an in-depth understanding of AI technology's potential and boundaries. While a flair for innovative solutions is valuable, successful AI PMs are pragmatic and focused, ensuring that each product in development is novel but also marketable and profitable.

As AI reshapes industries such as healthcare, finance, and entertainment, the need for adept PMs who can bridge the gap between traditional product management and AI-driven initiatives is crucial. In the following sections, I will detail how to leverage your existing skills and identify which new skills you need to master to be a successful AI PM.

Four buckets (shown in Figure 3-1) encompass the skills needed to be an AI PM: core product management craft and practices, engineering foundations, essential leadership and collaboration skills, and AI lifecycle and operational awareness. Each bucket has a list of relevant skills for the job. Whether you aspire to be an AI PM or just seek to sharpen your existing expertise, the insights shared here will guide you to the core skills and knowledge needed to stay sharp in the industry. In this chapter, consider how you will use these skills throughout the AIPDL.

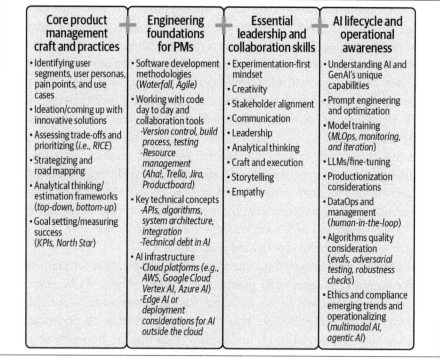

Figure 3-1. The different buckets of the AI PM skill set

Core Product Management Craft and Practices

This bucket discusses the core competencies that form the backbone of any successful PM's skill set. This section will confirm that much of an AI PM's responsibilities parallel those of a generic PM. So, in this section, prioritize understanding how these foundational skills translate into the context of managing AI-driven products. This understanding will enhance your effectiveness and ensure a smoother transition into the specialized field of AI product management.

A lot of these practices are covered in depth throughout the book. I've already discussed ideation and AI's unique superpowers in the previous chapter, and you will find more information on strategy and road mapping in Chapter 5. The goal of this section is not only to recap these fundamental skills, but also to guide you on how to amplify them with an AI perspective and bridge the gap between conventional product management practices and the novel demands of AI. This section aims to help you maintain and enhance your role in an AI-forward market.

IDENTIFYING USER SEGMENTS, USER PERSONAS, PAIN POINTS, AND USER NEEDS

Understanding your users is of the utmost importance. A proficient PM should be adept at breaking down their broader audience into distinct segments or personas. This granularity helps tailor product features to address specific needs or pain points. For an AI product, this might mean discerning and hypothesizing which user group will benefit most from a smart algorithm or which segment might need a more intuitive interface.

Specifically, user segmentation is the initial and critical step in understanding your audience. *User segmentation* involves dividing a more extensive user base into smaller, more defined groups based on shared characteristics. The ultimate aim is to refine product strategies to cater to these groups. To achieve this, one must analyze user data, which can encompass demographics, behavior on the platform, purchasing histories, or levels of engagement.

WRITING USER STORIES

User stories are a fundamental tool in product management. They serve as concise, straightforward descriptions of a feature from the end user's perspective. By centering the narrative on the user's needs and experiences, user stories ensure that product development focuses on delivering real value.

In AI, where the interplay between human requirements and machine functionality is intricate, user stories help maintain this balance. They compel the development team to consider the user's context in every design and implementation phase, fostering a user-centric approach that is crucial for the success of AI applications. Compelling user stories in AI also act as a bridge, translating complex technical possibilities into accessible benefits that resonate with users, thus driving greater adoption and satisfaction.

As an AI PM, crafting compelling user stories is even more critical. AI-driven solutions can be complex, often integrating advanced technologies that could easily drift away from practical user applications if not correctly anchored.

Here are some hypothetical user stories for various AI features that follow a particular three-line template:

- Who the user is
- What their use case is
- What their expectation or desired outcome is

Example 1: Improved recommendation system on Netflix

Story: Avoiding Repeated Recommendations

"As a Netflix viewer who often ignores specific show recommendations,

I want the system to notice that I'm not interested in that show and to stop suggesting it,

So that my recommendations are more relevant to my tastes."

Example 2: Peer recommendation feature for Spotify

Story: Peer Recommendations

"As a listener who trusts my friends' music tastes,

I want an option to see what songs my friends are currently listening to,

So that I can discover songs and playlists I will enjoy."

Example 3: Improved matching algorithm for a dating app such as Tinder or Bumble

Story: Deeper Interest Alignment

"As a user of a dating app who values shared hobbies and interests,

I want the matching algorithm to prioritize profiles based on mutual hobbies and core beliefs,

So that I can find matches with whom I have more in common, leading to potentially more meaningful connections."

Example 4: Personalized design template for an invitation on design software such as Canva

Story: Customized Invitation Templates

"As an event organizer looking to create unique invitations,

I want a system that generates personalized design templates based on the theme, color scheme, and tone of my event,

So that I can quickly create and send out appealing invitations and reflect the event's atmosphere."

Example 5: Self-driving safety feature enhancement for Tesla

Story: Advanced Safety in Varied Conditions

"As a Tesla owner interested in autonomous driving,

I want the self-driving car system to recognize and adjust to different weather and road conditions adaptively,

So that I can ensure a safer and more reliable autonomous driving experience in various environments."

Once the user story is defined, brainstorm the technologies and products to address user needs. The status quo is often insufficient in an ever-evolving tech landscape, particularly AI. AI PMs must think outside the box while developing ideas and tapping into creative solutions to address user needs.

Innovation keeps products relevant and competitive, whether it's a novel way of interacting with an AI-driven assistant or a groundbreaking algorithmic approach. We will discuss some innovation and problem-solving strategies in "Essential Leadership and Collaboration Skills" on page 67.

ASSESSING TRADE-OFFS AND PRIORITIZING IN AI PRODUCT MANAGEMENT

Not all features or solutions, even if feasible, should be pursued. One of the key responsibilities of an AI PM is to carefully assess trade-offs and prioritize decisions based on business goals, technical feasibility, and ethical implications. This process is not straightforward, because AI systems often present a unique set of challenges that require balancing multiple competing factors. Assessing trade-offs means weighing the benefits of one feature against its costs and potential risks, while always aligning decisions with the company's long-term strategy and user needs. Let's break down some of the common types of trade-offs faced during decision making.

Accuracy versus speed

In AI, particularly when designing systems that make real-time decisions, there is often a tension between the accuracy of an algorithm and the time it takes to process data. For example, in autonomous vehicles, object recognition algorithms must be accurate enough to detect pedestrians, vehicles, and obstacles. However, these algorithms also need to process that data in milliseconds to enable the car to make split-second decisions on the road. An AI PM must decide how much accuracy can be sacrificed to ensure that the system operates within the required time constraints. Too much emphasis on accuracy could delay the system's response, making it unsafe. Conversely, prioritizing speed without sufficient accuracy could lead to errors, compromising safety and trust in the technology.

Complexity versus simplicity

AI models range from highly complex, deep-learning networks to more straightforward, rule-based systems. Balancing complexity and simplicity often revolves around balancing ease of understanding and performance. For instance, in customer support chatbots, a complex NLP model might handle nuanced queries better, and give more humanlike responses. However, such a system can be harder to explain, debug, and maintain. Simpler models, on the other hand, may be more transparent and easier to troubleshoot but could fall short in performance. PMs need to decide if the added complexity is justified by the incremental improvements in user experience or operational outcomes.

Data quality versus quantity

AI systems are data hungry. However, there is a significant trade-off between gathering large volumes of data and ensuring that the data is of high quality, relevant, and ethically sourced. In fields such as healthcare, AI models require extensive patient data to improve diagnosis accuracy. However, ensuring that this data is accurate, properly labeled, and compliant with privacy regulations such as GDPR s critical. Collecting large amounts of low-quality or biased data can introduce problems that significantly undermine the model's performance. The role of the AI PM here is to ensure that the data pipeline is robust, and that the focus is not just on volume but also on the quality and ethical considerations of data collection.

Generalization versus specificity

One of the central dilemmas in AI development is deciding whether to build *general-purpose models* that can adapt to a range of tasks or *specialized models* optimized for specific tasks. For instance, in a recommendation system, a general-purpose model might provide suggestions across various domains (movies, books, music), but could lose some accuracy in each domain compared to a specialized model that only focuses on one domain, such as recommending movies. AI PMs must assess whether the broader reach of a general model is worth the potential loss in performance for more specialized needs or whether a suite of specialized models offers better results despite increased development complexity and cost.

User privacy versus personalization

As AI increasingly drives personalized experiences, PMs face tough decisions around user privacy. AI systems that analyze user data—such as targeted advertising platforms—are highly effective at providing tailored experiences, but they raise significant privacy concerns. Users are often concerned about how much personal data is being collected and how it is used, especially in light of tightening regulations such as GDPR. Striking a balance between delivering personalized experiences and safeguarding user privacy is paramount. In some cases, this trade-off might mean forgoing certain data-rich personalization features to maintain user trust, or investing in privacy-preserving AI techniques such as differential privacy.

Ethical considerations versus business goals

As AI systems become more sophisticated, ethical concerns around bias, fairness, and transparency are increasingly pressing. For example, in AI-driven hiring tools, PMs must ensure that the algorithms used to screen candidates are free from bias, ensuring fairness in the recruitment process. However, there may be business pressure to accelerate the hiring process, reduce costs, or meet specific quotas, which could tempt decision makers to overlook some of these ethical concerns. AI PMs must balance meeting business objectives with creating products that are fair, unbiased, and ethically sound, even if this means slowing down certain initiatives to mitigate risks.

Explainability versus performance

Another significant trade-off is between the performance of AI models and their explainability. Complex models such as deep neural networks or ensemble models may deliver higher accuracy but are often referred to as "black-box" models due to their lack of interpretability. In domains such as credit scoring and medical diagnostics, where the rationale behind a decision is critical, PMs must balance the need for high-performing models with the demand for models that can explain their decisions to users and regulators. A highly accurate model that cannot be explained may not be viable in environments where transparency and accountability are key.

BUILDING OR BUYING? STRATEGIC TRADE-OFFS

Beyond the technical trade-offs in model development, AI PMs also frequently face higher-level strategic trade-offs, particularly when, for example, we need to determine whether to build AI systems in-house or buy existing solutions. Here are key factors to consider:

Cost-benefit ratio

Building an in-house AI system offers more control and customization, but it's expensive and time-consuming. Buying a third-party solution may save time and resources, but it might not fully align with your business's specific needs or long-term strategy.

Expertise and talent

Developing AI systems requires specialized talent, such as data scientists and ML engineers. If your company lacks the expertise to build sophisticated AI models, you might opt to buy a solution or partner with external vendors. However, if AI is core to your business, investing in talent and building internally can provide a competitive advantage.

Time to market

Buying a prebuilt AI solution can drastically reduce the time it takes to bring a product to market, which might be critical in fast-moving industries. However, this may limit future flexibility, as prebuilt systems often lack the adaptability that in-house solutions can offer.

Risk and uncertainty

Building in-house often involves more risk due to uncertainties around data availability, model performance, and scalability. A ready-made solution mitigates these risks by offering a proven product, but it may introduce dependencies on third-party vendors.

Data privacy and ethics

Building an AI system internally allows full control over data handling and privacy protocols, which is critical for industries with strict regulatory requirements. A third-party solution may not offer the same level of transparency and control over how data is used and processed.

Scalability and maintenance

Buying a scalable solution can accelerate growth, but maintenance and customization may become an issue as your company evolves. Building internally allows for a solution that is scalable and tailored to your company's growth trajectory, but it comes with ongoing development and maintenance costs.

Competitive landscape

If AI is a core differentiator for your business, building an in-house system may provide a competitive edge. However, if AI is not central to your value proposition, buying a reliable, off-the-shelf solution might be the smarter, more cost-effective choice.

Alignment with core business goals

Ultimately, the decision to build or buy hinges on whether AI is central to your company's long-term goals. If AI is a key driver of innovation and competitive advantage, building in-house might be the better investment. If AI is a supporting technology, buying an external solution could be more efficient.

In reality, trade-offs aren't just about choosing between A or B; the contrast might not always be obvious. I like to think of the different factors almost like sliders in a 3D trade space that you need to position precisely, as discussed next in "Defining Your Trade Space". You can calibrate your approach across multiple dimensions.

DEFINING YOUR TRADE SPACE

Imagine you're building an AI-powered feature. Your trade space could involve any of the aforementioned trade-offs. To give a quick example, let's pick three trade-offs: balancing cost versus benefit, time to market, and risk versus reward. For this example project, you might decide that faster time to market is essential, which could mean choosing an off-the-shelf AI solution. But this choice might sacrifice some control and customization, pushing you to balance these losses by investing more in other areas, such as user experience or customer support.

This trade space isn't static. As your project evolves, so do the trade-offs. Early in development, you might prioritize quick wins, but as the project matures, long-term sustainability and scalability might take precedence. Visualizing your trade space as a dynamic, shifting landscape allows you to make more informed strategic decisions.

Your trade space will be unique to your product, your market, and your organization's goals. For example, a small startup might prioritize speed and agility, while a large enterprise might focus more on scalability and long-term ROI.

Here is my six-step guide to defining your own trade space:

1. **Step 1: Identify key factors**

   Start by listing the main trade-offs relevant to your product, such as the factors mentioned earlier. At the very minimum, you will want to include cost, time, expertise, and risk. Some trade-offs will be more obvious and common, such as balancing privacy with personalization, but there might be different trade-offs that you will need to capture on a case-by-case basis by talking to your stakeholders. Research scientists might bring up new factors that you haven't thought about; for example, aspects of the product that can be improved to ensure that the solution is robust and scalable and to keep computational costs low. It is a good practice to talk to your scientists, engineers, and UX designers to paint a full, accurate picture of your trade space.

2. **Step 2: Rank priorities**

   Determine the relative importance of each factor. What's non-negotiable? What are you willing to compromise on? Note that your stakeholders will have different goals. For example, stakeholder 1 might want to optimize for quality, whereas stakeholder 2 wants to optimize for time to market. Ultimately, you are responsible for painting the full picture by adding your vision and strategic thinking.

3. **Step 3: Map out interdependencies**

   Understand how each trade-off influences the others. For example, reducing cost might increase time to market or decrease customization. You will definitely need to talk to your scientist, engineering, and marketing/PR teams.

4. **Step 4: Visualize the trade space**

   Create a visual representation of your trade space, such as a matrix or graph, where you can plot different scenarios and outcomes, as shown in Figure 3-2.

5. **Step 5: Test different scenarios**

   Use this trade-space model to simulate different decisions and their impacts. Adjust your strategy based on these simulations.

6. Step 6: Iterate and adjust

As your project progresses, revisit your trade space regularly. Adjust your priorities and strategies as new information becomes available or as market conditions change.

Figure 3-2 is an abstract graph that visualizes the trade space with various constraints factored in. It can help you during ideation and decision making. To create a trade space, identify all relevant constraints (such as resources, ethics, technology, or regulations) and trade-offs for your problem, then map these constraints as boundaries to define a solution space, visualizing where acceptable solutions lie within these intersecting limits. Your solution follows somewhere in the solution space. Make sure to explicitly call out the risks and opportunities of each trade-off.

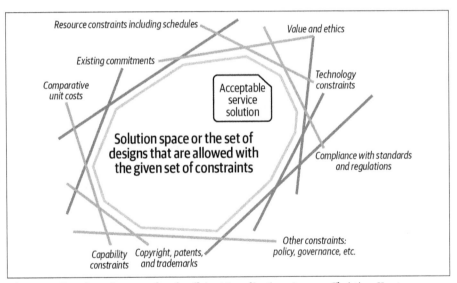

Figure 3-2. Sample trade space of trade-offs in AI applications (source: Christian Kaestner (https://oreil.ly/v6MTu))

INCORPORATING TRADE-OFFS IN A PRODUCT REVIEW

Determining the right path forward for complex AI solutions is a collaborative process that requires input from cross-functional partners and leadership. A product review is one of the most effective ways to align on trade-offs, constraints, and strategic priorities. Chapter 5 provides a detailed guide to conducting product reviews. In the Appendix, I introduce a template for crafting product reviews that you can use as part of the product review document. It's a good practice to include an executive summary at the top, with the goal of discussing the trade space with your leadership. These summaries are designed to present multiple options, their trade-offs, and recommendations in a clear, structured way to ensure informed decision making.

Table 3-1 provides an example of how I visually represent different solutions for an AI product, including key factors, trade-offs, and potential outcomes. The example depicted is for a decision between on-device processing and cloud processing that weighs key factors and their pros (+) and cons (–). For this hypothetical scenario, the factors I chose are User Experience, Ethics and Privacy, Compliance, Resource Constraints, and Technology Constraints.

Table 3-1. Executive summary example listing pros and cons of decision options

Factor	Option A: On-device processing	Option B: Cloud processing
User Experience	+ Fast response times (low latency), ideal for real-time applications. + Offline functionality ensures reliability in areas with poor connectivity. – Limited by device hardware, restricting model complexity.	+ Supports more advanced AI models with better accuracy and features. + Scales easily for multiple users without device limitations. – Dependent on consistent network quality; latency may impact experience.
Ethics and Privacy	+ User data stays local, improving privacy and reducing risks of breaches. – Higher risk of exposure if the device is lost or hacked.	+ Centralized oversight simplifies data auditing and security monitoring. – Data aggregation increases risk of misuse or regulatory violations.
Compliance	+ Easier to comply with strict regulations such as GDPR or HIPAA by keeping data local. – Device-based compliance may vary based on hardware and software partnerships.	+ Simplifies global compliance management by centralizing control. – Cross-border data flow restrictions may complicate deployment.

Factor	Option A: On-device processing	Option B: Cloud processing
Resource Constraints	+ Lower ongoing costs after the initial investment. – Significant up-front hardware investment to enable on-device processing.	+ Flexible pay-as-you-go pricing model reduces waste during idle periods. – Ongoing operational expenses for server infrastructure and cloud scaling.
Technology Constraints	+ Independent of network availability, ensuring robustness. – Requires lightweight AI models optimized for constrained hardware.	+ Supports cutting-edge AI models and technologies that demand high compute power. – Dependent on stable internet connections, which may create failure points.

After the table, add your recommendation and a justification. Visit the Appendix for the full product review template.

Setting a clear direction and charting a path are essential to ensuring a successful AI product launch and market acceptance. PMs define the strategic vision for the product, ensuring alignment with organizational goals. This involves laying out a road map and a visual representation of the product's journey over time, detailing what features to develop and when. Setting the strategic vision can also encompass milestones such as data acquisition or model refinement for AI products. I will discuss road mapping in detail in Chapter 4, which focuses on the day-to-day management of AI products.

How to Develop General Product Management Skills

The necessary skills to be a successful PM are constantly changing. For any successful professional, it is essential to keep learning and to brush up on existing skills. Recognizing the unique challenges and opportunities within AI product management, this section is structured to guide you through various educational and practical experiences that enhance your analytical reasoning, decision making, and hands-on capabilities, which are essential for thriving in this dynamic field. Here, you'll find actionable advice to start and continuously advance your journey in mastering the skills needed for effective AI product management.

EDUCATIONAL PURSUITS

AI PMs need a foundation built on educational pursuits that equip them with analytical and decision-making skills. Formal courses play a crucial role in this development. These courses range from broad classes focusing on analytical reasoning to more specialized ones explicitly tailored for the tech and AI sectors. Such educational offerings enhance critical thinking and provide you with robust analytical tools to effectively drive AI projects forward. You can take these courses at a traditional university or through online learning platforms such as Coursera *(https://www.coursera.org)*, edX *(https://www.edx.org)*, and Udacity *(https://www.udacity.com)*. These platforms offer specialized programs developed by experts in their fields, ensuring that learners can access cutting-edge knowledge irrespective of their geographic location.

HANDS-ON EXPERIENCE

Beyond formal courses, workshops and bootcamps offer practical, hands-on experience in a condensed format, making them an excellent way for you to deepen your understanding of specific areas, particularly in data analytics. Platforms such as Maven *(https://maven.com)* (where I teach), General Assembly *(https://generalassemb.ly)*, and Le Wagon *(https://www.lewagon.com)* host workshops that are highly regarded in the tech community for their focus on current industry practices and technologies.

In addition to bootcamps, participating in hackathons is another excellent way for AI PMs to gain hands-on experience while leveraging community knowledge and networking. Platforms such as Devpost *(https://devpost.com)* and Kaggle *(https://www.kaggle.com)* host numerous hackathons, offering opportunities to work on specific problems, often with datasets that mimic real-world scenarios. These events not only challenge participants to apply their skills under time constraints, but also foster a spirit of collaboration and innovation, providing a learning platform that is both competitive and educational.

Finding ways to engage in diverse projects is essential for AI PMs. PMs encounter challenges requiring innovative solutions and adaptive thinking by participating in various AI projects. This exposure enhances their problem-solving capabilities and deepens their understanding of different AI applications and their potential impacts. Such experiences are invaluable as they prepare AI PMs to handle real-world AI product development complexities.

CONTINUOUS LEARNING

The field of AI is remarkably dynamic, making continuous learning a cornerstone of success for any AI PM. Following breakthrough research, changing methodologies, and relevant industry news is essential. Regularly consult AI blogs from major tech companies, such as Meta's AI Blog (*https://ai.meta.com/blog*) and Google's AI Blog (*https://oreil.ly/bb_N_*), where people discuss new advances, research outcomes, and case studies. Additionally, subscribing to well-curated newsletters such as MIT Technology Review's *The Algorithm* (*https://oreil.ly/AWtWx*), *AI-Weekly* (*https://ai-weekly.ai*), O'Reilly's AI Newsletter (*https://oreil.ly/2SzI4*), and *Last Week in AI* (*https://lastweekin.ai*) can provide a steady stream of current and relevant information. These resources help you stay informed about the latest trends, cutting-edge technologies, and the competitive landscape to build strategies and tools for managing AI-driven products.

Essential Leadership and Collaboration Skills

As experienced product managers, you must possess various soft skills crucial for successful AI product management. This section builds on those existing abilities, focusing on how to adapt and enhance them for the specific challenges of managing AI products.

While technical knowledge in AI development is essential, the role of an AI PM also heavily relies on your ability to empathize with users and apply your interpersonal skills to bridge the complex gap between advanced AI technologies and practical, user-centric applications. Here, we'll dive into which soft skills are vital for AI PMs and how you can further develop these skills to effectively create and launch solutions that incorporate cutting-edge technology and that genuinely resonate with and meet the needs of your users. This approach will enable you to leverage your existing strengths to foster innovation and ensure that your AI products are as impactful and user-focused as possible.

CREATIVITY

Creativity empowers PMs to ideate unique solutions, envision novel product features, and think outside the box to meet user needs. In the rapidly evolving landscape where new capabilities and possibilities emerge faster than we can keep track of them, a creative approach can distinguish a successful product from a mediocre one. Creativity allows AI PMs to envision not just the immediate functionalities of a product, but also its potential to transform industries or even create entirely new ones. It's about seeing beyond the current technology to what could be possible, and making bold decisions that pave the way for innovation. To foster such creativity, you can immerse yourself in diverse experiences, from arts to travel, enhancing your ability to think outside the box. Regular brainstorming sessions, like those we discussed in Chapter 2, further stimulate creative thinking, making it a critical practice for innovation.

The following subsections explore different ways to channel creativity into the management of AI products, highlighting how creativity manifests in innovative problem-solving, product differentiation, and storytelling. By delving into these topics, you'll see that creativity is about more than generating 100 ideas; more importantly, it contributes to developing unique solutions, distinguishing your product in a competitive market, and effectively communicating its value.

Innovative problem-solving and design thinking

One of the primary ways creativity manifests in AI product management is through innovative problem-solving. Often, solutions aren't clear and they require outside-the-box ideas. Practicing design thinking is a great way to be a creative problem solver. The heart of practical design thinking involves empathizing with users, defining pain points, and testing to solve user-centered problems. Consider the example where you are an AI PM tasked with improving user experience and customer sentiment for public transportation. By creatively applying AI technologies to reduce the pain points from the frustration of wait times, you can create a valuable product that dramatically enhances the customer service experience.

Product differentiation

Creativity also plays a crucial role in product differentiation. A creative AI PM might integrate seemingly unrelated data sources to provide unique insights in a market crowded with AI solutions. For instance, an AI PM in the retail sector could innovate by combining weather forecast data with consumer purchasing patterns to predict and respond to changes in purchasing behavior due to weather conditions. Knowing how to deliver value and set a competitive advantage through differentiation is a creative challenge.

Storytelling

Storytelling is a strategy for securing stakeholder buy-in, fostering team cohesion, enhancing communication, and building a solid brand identity. By articulating a clear and compelling narrative, PMs ensure that everyone—from team members to stakeholders—aligns with the product's goals. This narrative approach helps build empathy toward users, facilitate better communication within teams, and create solutions that meet user needs. A consistent story that resonates across all user touchpoints establishes a memorable brand identity, making the product a part of the user's story.

Note

By fostering creativity, AI PMs ensure that they keep up with technological advancements and have a vision for the direction of innovation. They turn abstract ideas into tangible products that can significantly impact businesses and consumers, ensuring that their projects meet current market needs and shape future trends.

COMMUNICATION

Effective communication is crucial for translating complex AI concepts into clear, understandable narratives that resonate with stakeholders and users. For example, an AI PM should be able to effectively explain the benefits of a new AI algorithm to nontechnical board members, resulting in full project backing. You can develop this skill through regular interaction with diverse audiences. Practice breaking down intricate AI functionalities into simpler terms during team meetings, stakeholder presentations, and informal discussions. Not only will this ensure clarity, but it will also help build confidence in your ability to bridge the technical and business worlds.

LEADERSHIP

One of the core qualities of a successful leader is the ability to unify diverse teams around a shared vision. Leadership requires domain expertise and a profound understanding of the product's trajectory and goals. An AI PM will collaborate across various business functions and must bridge multiple departments—such as engineering, design, and marketing—to build alignment on the product vision and milestones. Collaboration is essential when integrating AI technologies into products loved by the masses. Meaningful and effective collaboration hinges on the PM's ability to lead teams to a common finish line.

To enhance leadership capabilities, an AI PM should actively pursue mentorship from experienced professionals in the industry. Mentorship offers invaluable insights into successful leadership strategies and equips managers with the tools to tackle the unique challenges of leading AI-focused initiatives. Mentorship can manifest in various forms, including one-on-one conversations, leadership workshops, and industry conferences.

ANALYTICAL THINKING

Analytical thinking is a cornerstone skill for AI PMs, empowering them to leverage data to aid decision making. I believe that data-driven decision making is paramount in any role. As a product leader, I am more confident in making decisions using relevant data from market due diligence or pilot experiments than from instinct or gut feeling. Begin by identifying key metrics relevant to your product's success. Use analytics tools or custom dashboards to track these metrics. Regularly review data trends and anomalies. When deciding, use A/B testing to determine the best course of action.

Develop a habit of questioning assumptions and backing decisions with data. While understanding how to interpret results from predictive models and simulations is of the utmost importance, a successful AI PM will also know the different types of ML models and the scenarios in which they are best deployed. For example, regression analysis is a simple model used to predict user behavior, and clustering techniques effectively segment users based on usage patterns. These data science methods help PMs evaluate the best approach to solving different aspects of a complex problem. A strong foundation in data analysis will help a PM find the right balance when faced with difficult trade-offs.

Enrolling in specialized courses focused on key data science concepts, such as statistical analysis, predictive modeling, and ML, is a great way to strengthen analytical skills. Many data science classes and curriculums are available in person and online. Educational platforms such as Coursera and the O'Reilly AI Academy (*https://www.oreilly.com*) are accessible and provide the latest methodologies in the field from many qualified industry professionals and scholars.

Of the many data science courses available, every aspiring AI PM should take classes on data analytics and visualization, statistics and probability, and ML and AI. These courses equip PMs with a robust analytical toolkit for effective decision making. PMs need basic technical skills to work effectively and discuss complex concepts and trade-offs with engineers and scientists. Knowledge of ML and AI technologies prepares managers to accurately understand the feasibilities and possibilities of the technology.

EMPATHY

At the heart of every AI product lies the user. Practicing empathy ensures that AI solutions are built with a deep understanding of user emotions, needs, and challenges. Great ways to polish this skill are to engage directly with users, conduct interviews, immerse oneself in user feedback, and regularly practice perspective-taking exercises to resonate with diverse user segments. We are looking for ways to make our lives better, and practicing empathy is the best way to learn about one another and find ways to be a team player. By establishing these soft skills, AI PMs can use novel technologies to build experiences that resonate with the users.

Next, I'll share the relevant engineering and AI-based knowledge that an AI PM must grasp quickly.

Engineering Foundations for Product Managers

Due to the technical complexity and ongoing evolution of AI technologies, a foundational understanding of engineering principles is especially critical for AI PMs. Basic engineering knowledge is crucial for effectively communicating with engineering teams and creating feasible and impactful product road maps. While this book won't go deep into the engineering foundations listed in Figure 3-1, the following overview will equip you with the necessary basics to enhance your collaborative efforts and understanding of AI product management.

WORKING WITH CODE

In this section, we will discuss why understanding coding practices is crucial for managing AI products. As AI technologies increasingly underpin product functionalities, AI PMs must possess a practical grasp of coding to effectively oversee development processes and ensure seamless integration of new technologies. I will break down the best coding practices for developing new AI-driven products. From understanding version control to recognizing clean code practices to appreciating the nuances of algorithm optimization, each subsection will build on the one preceding it to provide a comprehensive guide on how to work effectively with code. This knowledge facilitates better communication with technical teams and empowers PMs to make informed decisions that influence the product's technical strategy and execution.

Version control

Version control is pivotal for any collaborative project, and it's even more critical in code-extensive projects. Having a system to manage document changes is imperative to monitoring and storing documentation, and is even more important in minimizing risk from errors or unforeseen negative impacts from changes. Having a systematic version control tool allows cross-functional teams to collaborate more effectively. Systems such as Git (*https://git-scm.com*) enable teams to manage changes to source code over time, tracking who made what changes and when. These tools ensure that anyone can recall a prior software version at any time. Comprehensive version control systems allow for better bug tracking and feature development; for example, you can use Git to review the progress on specific features or to understand the impact of certain changes in the project's history. This tool is essential for individual accountability and enabling collaborative reviews and contributions through platforms such as GitHub (*https://github.com*) or GitLab (*https://about.gitlab.com*).

Build process

Understanding the product build process is essential for any PM to set and manage realistic project timelines and expectations. PMs must have a complete scope of the tools and processes used to build the product. Becoming familiar with the leading build systems and workflow optimizers is a great way to start. For PMs, processes and technologies used in the build are constantly improved, so expertise in new technologies is a continuous learning process for any PM. MLflow (*https://mlflow.org*) and Zapier (*https://zapier.com*) are popular GenAI build-process technologies.

MLflow plays a crucial role in managing AI model training and deployment complexities and is most frequently used to track experiments, package code into reproducible runs, and manage the deployment of models from various ML libraries.

Zapier is known for automating workflows by compiling, linking, and packaging them into executable products called *Zaps*, which use specific events in one app as triggers to perform tasks in another app, streamlining processes and boosting efficiency.

By understanding these tools, you can better anticipate delays or issues that might arise from dependencies or the integration of new code in your AI product, ensuring smoother project flows and more accurate scheduling.

Testing

Testing exists in all workflows. A thorough understanding of testing methodologies is crucial for ensuring the quality and robustness of the final product. Knowing the unit-testing frameworks pytest (*https://oreil.ly/wA8uM*) and TensorFlow (*https://oreil.ly/K_wHo*) can help you simulate different scenarios for AI models to test for the robustness and accuracy of AI-driven applications before they go into production. Unit tests are designed to test individual software components, ensuring performance in isolation.

For example, in an AI-driven application, unit tests might validate ML models' accuracy and response time under various conditions. This understanding helps you advocate for adequate testing phases and ensures that the product meets quality standards before it reaches customers.

Resource management

Computational resources can significantly impact the performance and costs of AI projects. Having robust resource management systems is imperative to effective and efficient resource allocation. Tools such as Kubernetes (*https://kuber netes.io*) and Docker (*https://docker.com*) are commonly used to manage server loads and optimize resource allocation efficiently. Kubernetes, for example, allows for automatically scaling applications based on the server load, which can be crucial for deploying AI models that may require significant computational power. Understanding these tools and principles enables you to make informed decisions about resource allocation, anticipate potential bottlenecks, and manage operational costs effectively.

Note

Understanding how your engineers interact with code and the models they build should give you a foundation to collaborate knowledgeably and build rapport with your technical team.

KEY TECHNICAL CONCEPTS

This section will explore fundamental technical concepts for managing AI products effectively. As AI continues to integrate into various industries, understanding these concepts will help you effectively oversee the design, development, and integration of AI technologies. This section provides a comprehensive look into the technical backbone of AI products, from the mechanics of APIs that facilitate seamless software interactions to the intricacies of algorithms that drive AI functionality. These concepts enhance a manager's ability to make informed decisions and enable effective communication with technical teams and stakeholders.

APIs

APIs are crucial for building connections between disparate software systems, making them essential for AI PMs who must integrate AI models with existing systems or third-party applications. Understanding APIs allows AI PMs to leverage external services and data and to make their own AI functionalities available in a way that other applications can easily consume. For example, an AI PM might oversee the integration of an ML model into a broader CRM system using

APIs to enhance predictive customer analytics. You can ensure seamless data exchange and functionality between disparate software components by understanding how APIs work, leading to more robust and versatile AI solutions.

Algorithms

Algorithms are the heart of what drives AI systems and experiences. An educated understanding of ML models such as regression models, neural networks, and reinforcement learning is important when building AI products. Knowing how these algorithms process data and learn from inputs allows AI PMs to decide which techniques best suit specific tasks. For example, understanding the differences between supervised and unsupervised learning algorithms[1] can help you choose the right approach for customer segmentation or anomaly detection tasks. This foundational knowledge not only aids in strategic product decision making but also enhances communication with data scientists and engineers. I provide a deeper dive into algorithms and the model-training process later in this chapter.

System architecture

System architecture affects every aspect of product development and deployment. *System architecture* refers to the structured design of the overall system that outlines how various software components, hardware elements, and integration with other systems interact to form a complete product. System architecture sets the foundation for the product's functionality, performance, and scalability. It ensures that all parts of the product work together cohesively and efficiently, meeting both the technical requirements and the user needs.

Knowing the ins and outs of the system architecture helps you design scalable and resilient products capable of handling increased computational demands. For instance, an AI PM must understand how to structure a system that integrates a real-time ML model without impacting the overall system performance.

---

1 *Supervised learning* is a type of ML in which models are trained using labeled data, allowing the algorithm to predict outcomes based on defined criteria. *Unsupervised learning* involves training models on data without labels, asking the algorithm to identify patterns and structures from the data itself.

Note

This detailed exploration of APIs, algorithms, and system architecture has underscored their critical roles in successfully managing AI products. By understanding how APIs enable interoperability between systems and comprehending the significance of robust system architecture, you will be better equipped to develop novel products that leverage the power of AI.

Software development methodologies

There are two popular development methodologies: Waterfall and Agile.

The Waterfall methodology (*https://oreil.ly/_nwjh*) is a traditional, sequential software development approach characterized by its linear and structured phases. This model divides the development process into requirements gathering, design, implementation, verification, and maintenance. Each phase must be completed before the next one begins, with little room for revisiting a phase once it's closed. While the Waterfall model provides a clear, predefined path that can simplify planning and execution, its rigidity is a notable limitation, particularly in projects requiring flexibility due to changing requirements or technologies. In environments where project specifications are unlikely to change and clarity is crucial from the outset, the Waterfall methodology can be highly effective.

The Agile methodology (*https://oreil.ly/xIkS9*) is a dynamic and collaborative software development approach designed to quickly accommodate change and deliver value. Unlike the Waterfall model, Agile breaks the project down into smaller, manageable increments known as *sprints*, typically lasting a few weeks. This approach emphasizes continuous planning, testing, and iterations.

Agile fosters a collaborative work pattern that highly values feedback. Feedback loops help ensure that the development aligns closely with user needs and that adjustments to a model can be made in real time. Agile's iterative nature allows for rapid releases and swift change, making it ideal for dynamic and uncertain environments.

Estimation frameworks

Estimation frameworks accurately forecast the time and resources required for various tasks and projects. This section looks at several frameworks and techniques that provide a high-level approach to planning.

Top-down estimation. This method starts with the overall scope of a project and estimates its total effort or cost based on past projects of a similar scale. Top-down estimation is particularly useful in the early stages of project planning when detailed information about the specific tasks and deliverables is unavailable. It's an effective approach for setting initial budgets, timelines, or project feasibility, especially when speed is a priority and the granular details are not yet defined. However, it may be less accurate for complex or highly detailed projects, as it makes generalizations that might not account for unique challenges or nuances.

Bottom-up estimation. Often used jointly with top-down estimation, *bottom-up estimation* (*https://oreil.ly/4lCT5*) involves breaking a project down into smaller, detailed components and estimating the effort for each before summing them to get a total project estimate. This granular approach allows PMs to assess the scope and needs of a project more accurately, considering specific factors and complexities of each component. By implementing bottom-up estimation, you can set realistic expectations and timelines, allocate resources more effectively, and mitigate the risks associated with project overruns.

Parametric evaluation. Another valuable technique is *parametric estimation* (*https://oreil.ly/tX6kT*), which relies on mathematical models and historical data to generate precise forecasts. By identifying key variables—such as cost per unit, time per task, or labor hours—and applying them to the scope of a project, parametric estimation provides a systematic way to assess resource needs. This approach is most effective when dealing with repetitive or scalable projects, where robust historical data and clear metrics are available. For example, in construction, manufacturing, or software development, parametric estimation can deliver reliable and consistent results. It's less suitable for one-of-a-kind projects or innovative tasks where historical data or clear metrics might be unavailable.

Expert judgment evaluation. Another widely used approach, *expert judgment estimation* (*https://oreil.ly/N4uh_*) involves leveraging the insights and experience of professionals with deep knowledge of the domain. Experts evaluate the scope, challenges, and requirements of a project to provide an informed estimate based on their prior experience with similar initiatives. Expert judgment is especially useful in scenarios where historical data is limited, the project involves innovation or unique elements, or the environment is uncertain. For example, when launching a novel product, developing a prototype, or managing a high-risk project, the nuanced perspectives of experienced professionals can help anticipate challenges and provide practical estimates. However, it's less ideal when objective, quantitative data is available and could provide greater accuracy or consistency.

Data analysis software

Data analysis software equips AI PMs with the tools to dive deep into data, enabling them to uncover patterns and derive actionable insights.

Python, with libraries such as Pandas (*https://oreil.ly/zwEhR*) and NumPy (*https://numpy.org*), is particularly popular for data manipulation and analysis capabilities. R (*https://www.r-project.org*) is another statistical software tool offering data analysis and visualization options and is ideal for more statistical work. SQL remains indispensable for efficiently querying large databases, allowing PMs to retrieve and analyze data directly from the source.

Additionally, visualization platforms like Tableau (*https://www.tableau.com*) transform complex datasets into understandable, interactive visual representations, facilitating more accessible communication of insights to stakeholders. Mastering these tools enhances your analytical capabilities to make data-driven decisions.

Note

While an AI PM doesn't need to be a seasoned engineer, foundational knowledge of these engineering principles and practices is indispensable. It ensures a more cohesive, informed, and efficient product development process, especially in the fast-paced, intricate world of AI.

The AI Product Development Lifecycle and Operational Awareness

Comprehending fundamental concepts such as ML algorithms, model training, fine-tuning, LLMs, model quality, and data management is crucial for effectively managing AI products. Grasping these concepts enables you to make informed decisions about designing, developing, and deploying AI systems.

Understanding ML algorithms helps you select the right approach to solve specific problems, while knowing model-training processes ensures that these algorithms perform optimally. You need to be able to assess model quality—this is essential to guaranteeing that AI products meet the required standards and deliver reliable predictions. Additionally, effective data management strategies are vital to maintain the integrity and efficiency of the data used for training AI models. These competencies form the backbone of successful AI product management, ensuring that products function efficiently and align with broader business goals and ethical standards. To understand these concepts, let's dive into the lifecycle of AI.

Chapter 2 introduced the AI Product Development Lifecycle and talked about the AI MVP. In this section, we'll take a closer look at the AIPDL. Understanding its stages is crucial, because they outline the path from an initial idea to a functioning AI product that can be iterated on and improved over time. Figure 3-3 shows the phases of the AI lifecycle. The lifecycle reiterates until the project reaches a fair minimum viable quality (MVQ), which represents the threshold at which the product provides sufficient value to address users' needs effectively and can be released to the market.

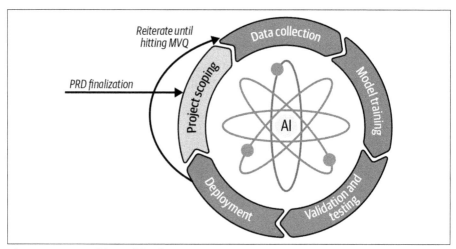

Figure 3-3. Stages of the AI lifecycle

PROJECT SCOPING

Before any development begins, you need to have a clear and actionable plan. This is where project scoping comes in. By this point, you should have a finalized PRD, as mentioned in Chapter 2, that defines the objectives, user needs, success metrics, and constraints of your AI product. *Project scoping* is all about the engineering team translating the product requirements into technical boundaries and expectations. What problems are you trying to solve? What outcomes are you aiming for? What data sources will be involved?

For example, if you're building an AI-powered personalized content recommendation system for a video streaming platform, the project scope might involve identifying key user interaction data to capture (such as viewing history, genre preferences, and watch duration) and setting a clear objective to increase user engagement by recommending relevant content. The PRD in this case would detail the types of data needed, the integration points with the existing platform, and the key performance indicators (KPIs) to measure success.

This phase also includes setting up initial alignment with cross-functional teams (engineering, data science, legal, design). Clear project scoping avoids scope creep and allows everyone to have a shared understanding of the project's goals and the path forward. It's a good practice to explicitly call out what is *out* of scope, which will help you set the right expectations for your cross-functional partners.

DATA COLLECTION

During the data collection phase, your scientist counterparts will have an initial plan for how much data is needed to train the model that will provide the desired output. In larger companies, an ML operations (MLOps) team is often responsible for gathering the necessary datasets that will feed into the AI models. The quality and diversity of the data you collect will directly impact the model's performance.

Here are some different sources from which you can acquire data:

- Internal databases
  - For personalized recommendation systems (such as a content streaming platform), collect *user activity data* such as clicks, search queries, watch history, or purchasing behavior.
  - Customer support chatbots can utilize *data from existing CRM platforms*, including past interactions, support tickets, chat logs, and customer profiles.
  - To optimize AI-driven business processes, use *internal operational data*, such as sales numbers, inventory records, transaction logs, or production metrics.
- Third-party APIs and platforms
  - Social media platforms such as X, Meta, and Instagram offer *APIs* that provide access to public posts, user profiles, hashtags, and engagement metrics. This is particularly useful for sentiment analysis and social media monitoring tools.
  - Government websites, educational institutions, and nonprofits often provide *free public datasets*. For instance, the US Census Bureau (*https://data.census.gov*), World Bank (*https://oreil.ly/DO_iQ*), and UN

(*https://data.un.org*) datasets are great sources for demographic, economic, and geographical data.

— *Weather and geolocation APIs* such as OpenWeather (*https://oreil.ly/AWkWL*) and Google Maps Platform (*https://oreil.ly/Bc-QR*) provide real-time weather conditions and location-based information, which can be integrated into various predictive models (such as for supply-chain forecasting or personalized marketing).

- User-generated content

    — Platforms such as Amazon (*https://www.amazon.com*), Yelp (*https://www.yelp.com*), and app stores have rich *datasets of user reviews, ratings*, and *comments*, useful for building sentiment analysis tools or recommendation engines.

    — You can collect direct feedback from users through *surveys, product feedback forms*, or *in-app feedback prompts* to gather insights into their preferences and behaviors.

- Public repositories and open source data

    — For image recognition or computer vision tasks, *image datasets* such as ImageNet (*https://oreil.ly/HBWTz*), COCO (Common Objects in Context) (*https://oreil.ly/OxXj7*), and Open Images (*https://oreil.ly/Bg8qF*) provide thousands of labeled images. For *video data*, YouTube and similar platforms can provide a source of labeled and unlabeled video content.

    — For NLP projects, *open text corpora* such as Wikipedia dumps, Common Crawl, news articles, and the Enron email dataset provide vast amounts of text for model training.

    — *Scientific and medical datasets* from medical institutions such as the National Institutes of Health (NIH) (*https://www.nih.gov*) and journal aggregators such as PubMed (*https://oreil.ly/JuXg8*) can be invaluable for training AI models in healthcare, such as diagnostic tools or patient risk assessments.

- Sensor and IoT data

    — Usage patterns and sensor data from *smart devices* such as smart refrigerators (e.g., temperature, humidity, and door sensors) and user interactions can be collected to train AI models for smart home systems.

— *Wearable devices* such as fitness trackers and smart watches provide data on factors such as physical activity, heart rate, and sleep patterns, which can be used to develop personalized health and wellness applications.

- Data vendors and marketplaces

  — Data marketplaces such as Kaggle (*https://www.kaggle.com*), Amazon Web Services (AWS) Data Exchange (*https://oreil.ly/DQarv*), and Data.gov (*http://data.gov*) provide access to a wide range of datasets, from consumer behavior to financial markets.

  — Commercial data providers such as Nielsen (*https://www.niel sen.com*), Experian (*https://www.experian.com*), and Acxiom (*https://www.acxiom.com*) sell data on consumer behavior, market trends, and audience demographics, which can be useful for targeted marketing and advertising models.

- Synthetic data generation

  — In cases where real-world data is scarce or sensitive (such as with medical data), you can generate *synthetic data* to simulate possible scenarios. This can involve creating artificial images for computer vision models, generating customer behavior scenarios for recommendation engines, or synthesizing voice data for speech recognition models. (This is a suboptimal data source and should be used as a last resort, when you lack better data or resources.)

When collecting user data, especially for products such as content recommendation systems or social media tools, you must ensure compliance with regulations like GDPR. This involves implementing robust safeguards to protect user information throughout the data handling process. The need for such measures stems not only from legal requirements, but also from the ethical responsibility to respect user privacy and trust.

Ensuring data protection serves several critical functions. First, it helps maintain user trust, a vital component of user retention and brand reputation. Users are more likely to engage with platforms that they believe handle their data securely and transparently. Second, compliance with data protection laws helps avoid significant legal and financial penalties that can arise from data breaches or misuse. These regulations require that data be collected for specified, explicit, and legitimate purposes and handled in a way that is secure, which minimizes the risk of breaches and misuse.

Moreover, ethical data use involves more than just compliance; it includes a commitment to fairness and nondiscrimination in automated decisions made by algorithms. This is particularly important in content recommendation and social media, where algorithms can potentially shape public opinion or impact individual behaviors. By adopting ethical data practices, companies ensure that their systems do not perpetuate biases or lead to unfair outcomes, thereby fostering a more inclusive digital environment.

Let's continue with the example of building a content recommendation system. In the data collection phase, you'd gather data from various sources, such as user behavior logs (clicks, watch history), content metadata (genres, directors, and actors), and user-generated information (ratings, reviews).

For a different example, if you were developing an AI image recognition tool for a social media app, you'd rely on open source image datasets, publicly available photos, or even user-uploaded content to build your dataset. This would involve collecting and manually labeling thousands of images into various categories to train the model to accurately identify objects in new images. The process might also include pulling data from image repositories.

Data collection is just the starting point. The value of data comes from how we label, classify, and make meaning out of information. In data science, the task of cleaning, labeling, and structuring data in a format suitable for model training is known as *data preprocessing*. This process starts with data cleaning. This involves removing or correcting inaccurate, incomplete, or irrelevant data points, which can significantly skew the outcomes of any analysis. Once we have a clean dataset, we continue to label data. By classifying data, we help the model learn to correctly identify input data. Moreover, classifying data into appropriate categories makes it easier to apply specific analyses and predictive models that require structured inputs. This classification might involve sorting data into predefined categories or creating new ones that better represent the underlying patterns and relationships.

Data collection and processing is not a one-time task; it's an evolving process. As you gather more user interactions or receive more content, you'll need to refine your data pipeline continually. As the environment changes and user behaviors evolve, routine updates to the datasets help ensure that models are trained on quality data.

MODEL TRAINING

Model training is the core phase of developing your product. This is where the magic happens, as your data is fed into the algorithms to create a model that can make predictions or provide insights. You need to embrace an experimental mindset, because you might try different algorithms, adjust hyperparameters, and evaluate initial performance to find the best approach.

At this stage, it's important to state the difference between an algorithm and a model in the context of data science and ML. While these terms are often used interchangeably, they refer to distinct concepts.

An *algorithm* is a set of rules that defines how to perform a task, in many instances, to make decisions. For example, decision trees, regression, and clustering are types of algorithms that describe the steps needed to solve a problem.

A *model*, on the other hand, is the specific use case of an algorithm that has been trained on data to solve a unique problem. A model is what you get when you feed data through an algorithm and allow it to learn from that data. It includes not only the algorithm's structure but also the optimized parameters that make predictions or decisions based on similar data to the ones it was trained on. For instance, a model might be a specific decision tree that classifies whether an image is a cat or a dog determined by learning from a set of training images.

While an algorithm can remain the same, different models can be developed from it by training on different datasets. This flexibility allows models to be optimized for unique business applications. For instance, if you're building a chatbot for customer support, you might start by training a simple NLP model using a dataset of past customer interactions. During this phase, you would select a relevant model (perhaps a transformer-based model, like GPT) and train it to understand and respond to various customer queries. You might need to revisit this step multiple times, tweaking the model to improve accuracy and relevance.

As an AI PM, understanding the basics of this phase and the trade-offs among the different approaches will help you communicate effectively with your data scientists. While you will never need to code as an AI PM, you will need to demonstrate AI awareness, especially when it comes to algorithms. At the end of this chapter you will find Figure 3-5, a map of AI algorithms and applications, to help you understand what goes into model training and algorithms.

VALIDATION AND TESTING

Once your model is trained, the next step is validation and testing. This phase is crucial because it determines how well your model generalizes to new, unseen data. You'll use separate validation datasets to test the model's accuracy, reliability, and overall performance.

For the content recommendation system, you might test the model by running it on a separate set of user data that wasn't included in the training phase. This will help you see how well the model can predict user preferences and identify any biases or gaps in its recommendations. Similarly, for the chatbot, validation might involve testing the model with a variety of real-world queries to see if it provides helpful, accurate responses.

Testing is an iterative process. You might find that the model doesn't perform as expected or that it introduces unintended biases. In these cases, you'll need to go back to the previous phase—model training—and refine your approach. The cycle of training, validation, and adjustment is repeated until the model meets the MVQ required to launch.

Setting the MVQ is a critical decision, and there's no single "right" or "wrong" threshold. As the PM, you determine this based on several factors, including user expectations, business goals, risk tolerance, and the specific use case of the AI product. For example, an MVQ for an AI-driven content recommendation system might be achieving a certain level of user satisfaction (often measured by qualitative metrics such as NPS and CSAT). In contrast, the MVQ for an AI medical diagnostic tool might require a higher threshold for accuracy to ensure patient safety, such as a 95% success rate in identifying a particular condition.

This iterative loop is key to building a robust AI product that provides reliable, valuable outcomes for users.

DEPLOYMENT

Once the model has been validated and meets the MVQ, it's time for deployment. Deployment is when the model moves from the development environment into a production environment and eventually goes live to the users. This step involves integrating the trained model into the product's infrastructure, setting up the necessary environments (such as cloud services and APIs), and ensuring that the model can interact with other system components effectively.

In our content recommendation system example, deployment would involve connecting the model to the streaming platform, where it can access user interaction data in real time to make personalized content suggestions. For the chatbot, deployment might mean integrating it with a company's customer support platform, allowing it to handle customer queries directly while learning from new interactions.

REMEMBER TO KEEP HUMANS IN THE LOOP

One "horizontal" aspect that cuts across all stages of the AI lifecycle is the necessity of keeping humans in the loop. While AI brings powerful capabilities, it's essential to remember that these systems function best when working alongside human expertise and oversight. Keeping humans in the loop ensures that your AI product not only learns from the data but also aligns with user needs, ethical standards, and business goals. Each stage of the AI lifecycle benefits from human involvement.

During the model-training phase, human input is crucial. Data labeling often requires human expertise, especially in complex domains such as medical imaging and financial analysis. Involving human experts helps ensure that the model is trained on accurate, contextually relevant data, reducing biases and errors in the outcomes.

In the validation phase, human evaluation is essential for interpreting results and understanding the model's strengths and limitations. Humans can identify subtle errors or biases that automated metrics might overlook, which is crucial for models deployed in high-stakes environments such as healthcare and autonomous driving.

Even after deployment, human feedback loops are necessary. AI products should allow users to provide real-time feedback on recommendations or decisions. This feedback can then be fed back into the data collection and model retraining phases, creating an ongoing cycle of improvement.

Figure 3-4 illustrates where human input fits into the AI lifecycle. You'll notice that human involvement isn't isolated to a single phase; rather, it's interwoven throughout the entire lifecycle. This ongoing collaboration ensures that the AI product remains adaptable, ethical, and aligned with user needs.

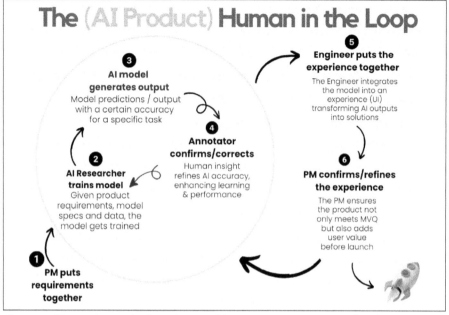

Figure 3-4. Human interaction in each stage of the AIPDL (source: Dr. Marily Nika)

MAPPING AI ALGORITHMS AND APPLICATIONS

I often say that AI is not a product. Rather, it's a suite of technologies and methodologies that empower a wide range of products and solutions across various industries. The map I created, shown in Figure 3-5 (larger version available online (*https://oreil.ly/KDanI*)), provides an overview of how these technologies converge to create impactful and innovative applications. We'll explore the map, moving from core concepts to practical applications, to see how AI components integrate into real-world scenarios.

This map will help you understand what kind of AI *superpower* enables what kind of *AI-powered user experience*. There is, of course, no one-size-fits-all recipe, and there is significant overlap in these categories. However, my hope in creating this for you is to help you map out the different types of learning methods, algorithms, applications, use cases, and real-world examples. Please note this is not meant to serve as an engineering resource, and there are really infinite ways to visualize this, so I am not optimizing for accuracy, just for knowledge sharing (and fun!).

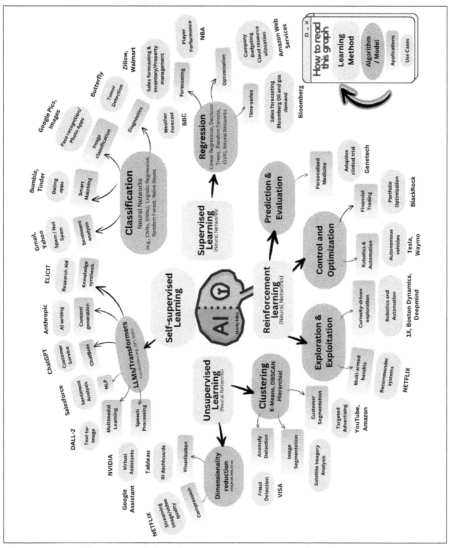

Figure 3-5. AI applications and algorithms map (source: Dr. Marily Nika)

Let's break down these categories:

Learning method

The term *learning method* in AI refers to an approach or technique used to train an ML model. This method determines how a model learns from data to make predictions or decisions.

Algorithm or model

An *algorithm* in AI is a set of rules or instructions designed to perform a specific task or solve a particular problem. A *model* in AI is a specific implementation of an algorithm that has been trained on data to predict outcomes or understand patterns. (I've bundled these two concepts due to their intertwined nature.)

Applications

The term *application* refers to the practical use of an AI model or algorithm to perform specific tasks that are valuable in real-world scenarios, or in other words, the AI product itself.

Use cases

You know what a *use case* is: how a product or feature can solve a problem or fulfill a need for its users. It's a scenario in which AI technology can be applied to solve a problem or enhance a process in a specific context.

This is a high-level graph that maps algorithms to use cases from a product perspective, purely for illustrative purposes. The reality of AI product development often involves a more nuanced and complex interplay between different algorithms and use cases.

Let's start by looking into each of the foundational AI learning methods that form the quadrants of the map: supervised learning, self-supervised learning, unsupervised learning, and reinforcement learning.

Supervised learning

Supervised learning involves training a model on a labeled dataset, which means that each piece of data in the training set is paired with the correct answer or outcome. This is the most common type of learning used in AI and it is suitable for a wide range of applications, from image recognition to predicting consumer behavior. It requires a substantial amount of labeled data and is generally used where the outputs are known and need to be predicted based on new inputs.

Supervised learning is suitable for classification tasks, such as the following:

Sentiment analysis
Analyzing text data from reviews or social media to determine their sentiment (positive, negative, neutral)

Smart matching
Using AI to match users or products in services such as dating apps or job portals based on learned preferences

Image classification
Identifying objects within an image and categorizing them into predefined classes

Diagnostics
In healthcare, using image data to diagnose diseases from scans or tests

It is also helpful for regression tasks, including the following:

Forecasting
Predicting future values such as sales or stock prices based on historical data

Optimization
Adjusting inputs to maximize or minimize certain outcomes, useful in logistics and resource allocation

Time-series analysis
Analyzing time-ordered data points to predict future points or trends

There are many applications and use cases for supervised learning models. For example, logistic regression and decision trees have become essential tools across various industries, with financial services being one of the most prominent adopters. These models are particularly effective in fraud detection, where they are trained on preclassified historical data—transactions that have already been labeled as either fraudulent or legitimate.

By analyzing this data, the model learns to identify subtle patterns and anomalies that may suggest fraudulent activity. For example, if a credit card transaction differs significantly from a customer's typical spending habits or takes place in an unexpected geographic location, the system can flag it for further review. This predictive capability helps protect both consumers and financial institutions, reducing losses and contributing to a more secure banking experience. Similarly, healthcare companies apply supervised learning in medical diagnostics, especially through image classification techniques. These models can analyze medical images, such as scans or X-rays, to help diagnose diseases, offering invaluable support to healthcare professionals in delivering accurate and timely care.

Self-supervised learning

Self-supervised learning is a type of ML in which the system learns to understand data by itself, without explicit labels provided by humans. Instead, it generates its own labels from the data by predicting missing parts or properties of the data. LLMs and transformers are crucial in self-supervised learning for understanding and generating humanlike text. These models, trained on vast amounts of unlabeled text data, can predict text continuation and generate coherent pieces of text. Self-supervised learning is especially useful for tasks such as natural language understanding, where labeled data can be scarce or expensive to produce.

Self-supervised learning performs functions such as the following:

Speech processing
  Used to develop models that can transcribe speech without needing labeled data, by predicting the next word or sound in sequences

Multimodal learning
  Involves training models to process and integrate information from different types of data, such as text and images, to perform tasks like automatic captioning

NLP
  Used extensively to improve language models that power applications such as sentiment analysis and language translation

Its applications and use cases include the following:

Chatbots
  Utilizing advanced NLP capabilities, helps chatbots generate more relevant and context-aware responses

Content synthesis
  Enables the automated creation of content, such as articles and reports, that feels natural and humanlike

Unsupervised learning

Unsupervised learning involves training a model on data that has not been labeled, annotated, or classified. The model learns without any guidance, finding patterns and relationships in the input data. This method is crucial for discovering hidden patterns or intrinsic structures within data. It is often used for clustering, association, and dimensionality reduction tasks in datasets where we do not know the outcome in advance.

Unsupervised learning is strong at clustering tasks, such as the following:

Anomaly detection
Identifying unusual patterns or outliers in data, useful in fraud detection

Image segmentation
Dividing an image into multiple segments based on the similarity of pixels

Customer segmentation
Grouping customers based on purchasing behavior or preferences to tailor marketing strategies

It also helps in dimensionality reduction tasks such as these:

Compression
Reducing the size of data while maintaining its essential features, crucial for storage and analysis

Visualization
Transforming high-dimensional data into visual formats that are easier to understand and analyze

Applications and use cases for unsupervised learning include the following:

Anomaly detection
Identifying fraudulent credit card transactions

Customer segmentation
Enhancing user recommendations and targeted advertising

Reinforcement learning

Reinforcement learning (RL) is where an *agent*, a decision-making entity that takes actions to achieve a goal, learns by interacting with its environment and receiving rewards or penalties based on its actions. Neural networks and deep learning enhance RL by processing complex data inputs, allowing the agent to learn more sophisticated strategies. Neural networks and deep learning are key components in RL, especially in complex scenarios such as autonomous driving. *Neural networks*, structured like the human brain, consist of interconnected layers that process information. *Deep learning* uses multiple layers to enable sophisticated decision making.

RL is good for prediction and evaluation tasks such as personalized medicine, which involves tailoring healthcare treatments to individual patients based on predicted outcomes from different treatment plans. It is also strong for control and optimization tasks such as the following:

Financial trading
Using AI to make buy or sell decisions in real-time trading scenarios

Robotics and automation
Programming robots to perform tasks independently in manufacturing or service environments

Exploration and exploitation tasks aided by RL include the following:

Multi-armed bandits
A problem setup in which an algorithm must choose among multiple options with uncertain returns, optimizing for maximum reward

Curiosity-driven exploration
Encouraging AI systems to explore new or less-understood environments or datasets to improve learning

Applications and use cases for RL include the following:

Netflix
Uses multi-armed bandit algorithms (*https://oreil.ly/qwFQf*) for personalized viewing recommendations

Autonomous vehicles
Use deep learning and neural networks to process real-time data from cameras and sensors, helping the vehicle navigate safely by recognizing pedestrians, vehicles, and traffic signs

RL algorithms
    Empower robots to explore and perform tasks autonomously in manufacturing and service environments

RESPONSIBLE AI PRACTICES

Responsible AI practices are essential for ensuring that AI technologies are developed and deployed in ways that prioritize human welfare, fairness, and transparency. For AI PMs, this means embedding ethical considerations into every stage of the product and AI lifecycle. Lead your team by asking critical questions such as "Who will this product impact?" and "What potential harms might arise?"

When you identify potential risks, leverage ethical frameworks such as FATE (*https://oreil.ly/2__Yz*) (fairness, accountability, transparency, ethics) and the AI Ethics Canvas (*https://oreil.ly/v5YYH*) to guide the choice of algorithms, data collection methods, and model architectures. Don't stop there; be sure to monitor product performance and social impact metrics to detect and correct bias, errors, or misuse of the product in real-world settings. Regular audits and updates to the model based on ethical guidelines and user feedback are necessary to maintain responsible AI practices throughout the product's lifecycle.

Proactively identifying risks in AI systems is critical to preventing unintended societal harms, which can range from algorithmic bias to violating privacy and perpetuating stereotypes. You can conduct various risk assessments by evaluating the fairness of datasets, testing for potential biases in model outputs, and conducting scenario analysis to identify unintended use cases. For example, an AI-based hiring tool could unintentionally favor certain demographics if the training data is skewed, leading to discriminatory hiring practices. Similarly, a predictive policing algorithm might disproportionately target minority communities if trained on historically biased data. These risks, if unaddressed, can lead to public backlash, loss of trust, and even regulatory penalties.

You can mitigate these risks by creating diverse datasets. AI models are only as good as the data they are trained on, and ensuring that datasets represent a wide range of demographic, geographic, and contextual diversity is essential to minimizing biases. For example, a face recognition system trained predominantly on images of lighter-skinned individuals may fail to accurately identify darker-skinned individuals, leading to inequitable outcomes. To ensure robustness, AI PMs should stress-test the product using a wide array of edge cases.

Ethics and compliance

Compliance isn't just about checking boxes; it's about ensuring that AI products are trustworthy, are ethical, and meet the legal standards that protect users. This means you and your team must prioritize how data is collected, stored, and used; especially when handling sensitive information. The best practice is to anonymize, encrypt, and limit data collection and usage to only what is absolutely necessary to power the product. There are various policies that set guidelines for ethical AI practices. Proactively accounting for regulations such as GDPR and the AI Act ensures that the products are designed to be transparent and robust.

Explainable AI (XAI)

XAI is about designing AI systems to be easily understandable to the people who use them. At its core, it ensures that AI decisions don't feel like they're coming out of a "black box," where the user doesn't know why or how the system reached the decision it provided. XAI is especially important when designing AI products for high-risk situations; for instance, doctors diagnosing patients, financial advisors assessing risk, or customer service systems that interact with users directly. People need to trust the technology. That trust hinges on understanding not just what the AI decided, but also how it got there.

Making AI explainable means implementing methods that can break down algorithms and decisions into human-friendly explanations. For instance, feature importance scores can highlight which factors mattered most to the AI in making a prediction, such as showing that a patient's age and medical history were key in suggesting a diagnosis. Visualization tools, such as decision trees or heatmaps, can also help demystify the inner workings of complex models. Counterfactual explanations are another useful strategy to communicate what would need to change to achieve a different outcome; for example, "If your income were $5,000 higher, your loan application would be more likely to get approved." These methods make AI decisions more transparent, helping users and stakeholders understand what's happening under the hood.

But explainability isn't just about the user; it's a key component for the teams building the technology. Engineers and data scientists rely on XAI techniques to debug and refine models. If something goes wrong, like the AI making biased predictions, explainability tools can quickly pinpoint the issue. XAI practices reduce development risks and help ensure that AI systems comply with ethical guidelines and regulatory requirements.

Conclusion

This chapter discussed the essential skills required for managing an AI product, covering the spectrum from general project management principles to the specific technical knowledge of AI. We explored crucial AI concepts such as ML algorithms, model training, model quality, and data management—each vital for developing, deploying, and maintaining reliable and effective AI systems. The discussions highlighted the importance of understanding these technical elements, the need for adherence to ethical standards, and the value of transparency in building user trust.

The concept of a solution trade space highlights the importance of making informed strategic decisions that account for multiple interconnected factors. By defining your unique trade space, you can more effectively navigate the complexities of AI product development, ensuring that your final product is innovative and aligned with your long-term goals.

After establishing the multifaceted skill set required by AI PMs, it's clear that this role demands a unique blend of technical acumen and broad management skills. This role acts as the crucial link between AI's technological capabilities and users' real-world needs, ensuring that AI solutions are both impactful and sustainable. In Chapter 4, we will take a closer look at what a typical day in the life of an AI PM entails, providing a practical perspective on how these skills are applied to navigate daily challenges and opportunities in the field.

4

The AI PM's Day-to-Day

I hope it's clear to you by now that the central role of an AI PM is to orchestrate AI innovation and seamlessly integrate it into user experiences. But let's put that role into the broader context of an organization. Where exactly do you fit in as an AI PM, and how will your responsibilities shift as you move up the ladder?

The AI PM Career Ladder

A successful AI product strategy hinges on aligning the AI product vision and road map with the company's overall business objectives. The work of AI PMs can vary significantly depending on their level within the organization. This brings us to Figure 4-1, a high-level map of AI product management tasks across different levels inspired by larger organizations. As you explore it, identify where your current role aligns to understand what a successful product approach could look like for you and your team. Keep in mind, however, that these levels are meant for illustrative purposes. Roles and responsibilities can vary widely from company to company, and your specific role may be a blend of several management levels.

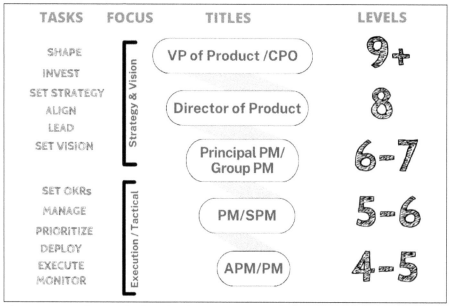

Figure 4-1. Map of AI PM levels and tasks (source: Dr. Marily Nika)

Let's break down what we see in Figure 4-1. The left column outlines the different levels within AI product management, ranging from hands-on execution at levels 4 and 5 to company-wide strategy at levels 9 and above, as well as the tasks and strategic focus for each.

Figure 4-2 complements the information shown in Figure 4-1 by breaking down the scope and focus areas for each level in more detail. For example, at levels 4 and 5, the emphasis is on monitoring AI model performance and ensuring data quality. This reflects the on-the-ground nature of execution-level roles. As you move up, the focus shifts to developing strategy, prioritizing use cases, and managing the AI deployment pipeline, indicating a transition toward shaping how AI will drive business goals.

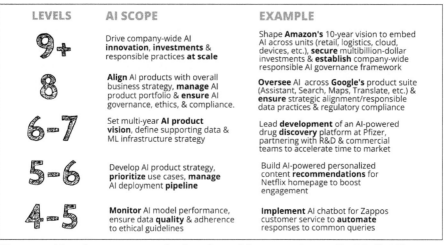

LEVELS	AI SCOPE	EXAMPLE
9+	Drive company-wide AI **innovation, investments** & responsible practices **at scale**	Shape **Amazon's** 10-year vision to embed AI across units (retail, logistics, cloud, devices, etc.), **secure** multibillion-dollar investments & **establish** company-wide responsible AI governance framework
8	**Align** AI products with overall business strategy, **manage** AI product portfolio & **ensure** AI governance, ethics, & compliance.	**Oversee** AI across **Google's** product suite (Assistant, Search, Maps, Translate, etc.) & **ensure** strategic alignment/responsible data practices & regulatory compliance
6-7	Set multi-year **AI product vision**, define supporting data & ML infrastructure strategy	Lead **development** of an AI-powered drug **discovery** platform at Pfizer, partnering with R&D & commercial teams to accelerate time to market
5-6	Develop AI product strategy, **prioritize** use cases, **manage** AI deployment **pipeline**	Build AI-powered personalized content **recommendations** for Netflix homepage to boost engagement
4-5	**Monitor** AI model performance, ensure data **quality** & adherence to ethical guidelines	**Implement** AI chatbot for Zappos customer service to **automate** responses to common queries

Figure 4-2. AI product management levels, tasks, and focus areas (source: Dr. Marily Nika)

EXECUTION-LEVEL AI PRODUCT MANAGEMENT (LEVELS 4–6)

We start at the execution level, which typically includes associate product managers (APMs) up to group PMs. If you find yourself in this layer, your focus is on the day-to-day development and deployment of AI products and features. You're the one working closely with AI/ML engineers and data scientists, tracking progress, removing roadblocks, and shipping AI capabilities. At this stage, your work revolves around setting Objectives and Key Results (OKRs), identifying product–market fit, and pushing through the product development cycle.

Look at the tasks listed in Figure 4-2 for levels 4 through 6. Here, you see responsibilities such as monitoring AI model performance and ensuring data quality—key areas where execution-level AI PMs spend much of their time. For example, if you're building a personalized content recommendation system (as we briefly discussed in Chapter 3) for a platform like Netflix (as mentioned in the figure), your work will involve close collaboration with engineers to develop, test, and refine the algorithms that drive those recommendations.

AI/ML PRODUCT MANAGEMENT (LEVELS 5–7)

Moving up a bit, AI/ML PMs play a critical role in defining product requirements, prioritizing the road map, and coordinating execution. They are responsible for driving individual AI product development from ideation through to deployment. Here, your job extends beyond simply building the product; it involves understanding the business goals and translating them into actionable AI strategies.

According to Figure 4-2, at levels 6 and 7 you start setting the multiyear AI product vision and defining the supporting data and infrastructure strategy. Take the example of Pfizer leading the development of an AI-powered drug discovery platform (*https://oreil.ly/NHoxe*); this kind of role requires aligning the AI product strategy with research and commercial teams, ensuring that the AI platform accelerates time to market. It's about balancing technical capabilities with long-term business objectives.

STRATEGIC LEADERSHIP (LEVELS 8+)

As you rise in seniority, your responsibilities shift from hands-on product development to setting the product strategy and leading the organization. Working at Meta and Google, I've observed how big tech companies have trended toward consolidating roles. The ladder becomes shorter as companies focus on having a small number of senior leaders who define the product direction and vision (top layers) and select managers who handle execution (bottom layers).

When you hit levels 8 and above, the focus is on aligning AI products with the overall business strategy and managing an entire AI product portfolio. This involves a lot of cross-functional work, ensuring that AI efforts are strategically aligned with company goals, governance policies, ethics, and compliance. For example, Google oversees its AI initiatives across a diverse suite of products (Assistant, Search, Maps, Translate, etc.), ensuring that data practices align with regulatory standards.

At the very top (levels 9+), you may step into roles such as head of AI Product or chief AI officer. In positions such as these, you're not just managing individual products. You're shaping the entire company's AI vision at scale. This level of leadership involves embedding AI across all units of the company, securing multibillion-dollar investments, and establishing company-wide responsible AI governance frameworks. The responsibilities here include ethical considerations, ensuring that data practices are compliant, and maintaining the integrity of AI models. The difference between these levels isn't just in scope; it's also in the strategic mindset required.

By understanding these levels, you can better map out where you currently stand and where you might want to go. Maybe you're at the execution level, working closely with engineers to build AI-driven features. Or perhaps you're moving toward shaping an AI product vision that aligns with the company's broader strategy.

The key takeaway is that your role as an AI PM will evolve, expanding from developing specific features to setting company-wide AI initiatives. But remember, these levels and responsibilities are a guide, not a strict hierarchy. Your journey might look different depending on your organization's structure and goals.

AI Product Manager Profiles

In this section, I invited some AI product leaders I admire to answer three questions that showcase the breadth and diversity of backgrounds and skill sets that I see every day in this profession. I hope these stories inspire you to pursue this path, regardless of your background.

ETHAN COLE

Ethan Cole is president of the Product Managers Association of Los Angeles and an alumnus of the AI Product Bootcamp.

What was your path to AI product management?

My path to product management was unorthodox. I'm a trained archaeologist and earned my PhD studying changes in human behavior in ancient Mexico and Peru. In those cultures, knowledge was power. For instance, the Maya were able to accurately predict solar eclipses, but the information was held in the hands of a few elites. Their ability to tell the populace that next week during the middle of the day, the sun would disappear and the stars would come out, and it actually happened, was enough for the townspeople to believe that their leaders spoke with the gods and validated their power.

The advent of smartphones democratized knowledge in a way that was never before possible. All of a sudden we all had access to all of the world's knowledge, wherever we are, 24/7, and basically for free (or at least it's available for the masses).

Recognizing that we were entering a watershed moment in human history, I elbowed my way into a startup and became a Mobile product manager. The advances we are seeing with AI, and generative AI specifically, feel like we are entering another watershed moment, which is why I leaned hard into the growing field of AI.

Describe a day in your life as an AI product leader.

I spend many of my days spreading awareness about the current capabilities of AI for product management, and the potential impact on the future. In only a few short years, AI has changed the game for product managers. Right now it's impacting not only what people are building, but how they are building. In 2023 and 2024, most companies have focused on integrating some aspect of AI into their products, largely to fulfill consumer demand and expectations. This has caused a number of folks in the field to contemplate new trade-offs in their product decision-making process, such as speed versus accuracy.

As I'm writing this in mid-2024, AI has made small improvements to product managers' daily tasks, from leveraging ChatGPT to help create user stories, to summarizing meeting notes and quickly translating them into Jira tasks. It's a cliché at this point, but an AI-enabled product manager will beat out one who doesn't leverage AI. Ironically, those who are not keeping up for fear that AI will replace them may actually be the first to go.

What do you want people coming into the field to know?

My advice for someone who is coming into the field is to lean in. We are still very much in the infancy of AI's impact on software development, product development, and our lives in general.

In early 2023, there were only a handful of folks who were truly experienced in AI product management (Marily Nika being one of them). As of mid-2024 there are more, but few with more than a year under their belt. A mentor of mine once provided sage advice: "If you focus on a new field, you can quickly find yourself becoming a top voice."

AI has already made significant impacts on our personal and professional lives. It will only continue to do so, likely at a pace the likes of which we have never seen. Earlier in human history tens of generations could go by with little or no technological innovations. The tectonic shifts in AI are moving so rapidly that every six months, fundamental changes are coming out. There's never been a more exciting time to build digital products. We are literally shaping the future!

MARK CRAMER

Mark Cramer is senior AI/ML product
manager at Stanford University.

*What was your path to AI product
management?*

My path to AI product management is perhaps circuitous. I have
an electrical engineering degree
and began my career as an engineer but, after a couple years, went
to business school. I felt isolated
as an engineer and desired a role
with more human interaction, so I went into business development and
sales. That, however, turned out to be too much human contact, and I
missed the technology. After a few years I settled into product management, which I feel has been an excellent fit for my skills and personality.

After founding a company with a heavy algorithmic focus (we built
technology that significantly improved the relevance of Google's search
results), I really returned to my roots. I got back into programming and
then, in 2017, ran across an ad on Facebook for a "deep learning nanode-
gree" from Udacity. I had no idea what a neural network was, but signed
myself up on impulse. I was hooked from the first lesson.

I continued to pursue online coursework while experimenting on my
own. This eventually led to an AI product management role at PARC,
the famed research and development laboratory. One of my interviewers
mentioned he was impressed by my initiative, so I'm confident this is what
got me the job.

Nevertheless, because of my passion for AI and desire to deeply understand the material, I sought ways to continue learning. One day, while
staring at Hoover Tower out my office window, I decided to see what
programs Stanford might have. A couple years later I received my Graduate
Certificate in AI and am now a TA in the program. I also moved to Meta
where, as an ML product manager, I've been as close to the cutting edge as
anyone could hope to be.

Describe a day in your life as an AI product leader.
My product management responsibilities at a previous company ran the gamut, from flying around the country to interview prospective customers to working with engineering and design to spec out the PRD. The breadth of the experience was extraordinary and exhilarating. With respect to the AI, however, I spent considerable time with ML research scientists to understand the limits of what was possible as well as conceive a value proposition that would work in an MVP.

My biggest learning might be how difficult it is to scope an MVP for an AI product. I've since spoken about this at several conferences. The most substantial hurdle in Andrej Karpathy's "software 2.0" world is that you cannot "know," *a priori*, how your application will perform.

Its behavior will depend on many factors, including the volume and quality of the training data. Models in practice can diverge significantly from theory, and many users won't have the patience to train the systems themselves. It's difficult to judge without significant experience, so I advise ML product managers to take great care when defining any MVP that's based on an ML model.

That being said, in the end we pulled together the necessary ML components, sufficiently trained on available data, to launch a product that delivered considerable value to our beta partners.

DIEGO GRANADOS

Diego Granados is cofounder of AI Product Hub, AI/ML product manager at Google.

What was your path to AI product management?
My path into AI was by "accident." In 2019 I was admitted to Georgia Tech's master's program in computer science, and at the same time, I was interviewing with Microsoft for a product manager role that was 90% typical PM role and 10% AI and ML.

Three months after I joined this new role at Microsoft, we were reorganized into a 100% AI and ML team. At that time, Kaggle, my classes at Georgia Tech, and working closely with data scientists on my team helped me understand and navigate the complexities of the world of AI and machine learning.

Describe a day in your life as an AI product leader.

As an AI product manager, I spend part of my day doing what any other PM would do: working on product requirements documents, looking at data, talking with customers, and checking progress with the engineering and data science team.

What makes my days unique is that I spend time understanding data that we'll use for our experiments and brainstorming with the data scientists on experiments and metrics, as well as meeting with other stakeholders who want to use machine learning in their products/features. With them, I spend my time understanding the problems they are trying to solve and whether we need machine learning to solve them.

One of the biggest differences in being an AI and ML PM is that, at the beginning of a new project, you spend time looking at what data you'll use, finding (ideally) responsible AI frameworks to guide your development, understanding whether you really need AI and ML, and thinking about how you and your users will understand and interpret the data.

What do you want people coming into the field to know?

Most product management skills are transferable, but for AI and ML, it's important to understand the technical aspects of machine learning as well as the principles of when and how you need to think about AI and ML for your product.

To learn the technical details, Kaggle is a great resource. To learn business- and product-related topics in machine learning, AI Product Hub (*https://www.aiproduct.com*) is a fantastic place!

JACLYN KONZELMANN

Jaclyn Konzelmann is director of Product Management at Google AI Labs and founder of YC S13.

What was your path to AI product management?

My path to AI product management has been fueled by a lifelong passion for building. Even during my university years, while pursuing my mechatronics engineering degree at Waterloo, I was drawn to hands-on projects, starting companies and organizations—at one point even designing conveyor systems for the Toronto airport through my own consulting practice. This drive to create continued after graduation, leading me to a role as a PM at Microsoft, where I honed my skills on Outlook. But my heart remained in 0-to-1 environments. That's why I launched a startup; it ended up going through Y Combinator, and I learned a lot.

While the company inevitably wound down, the experience led me to the Bay Area, where I went back to my PM roots, joining a growing company and helping to build their product team while reporting to one of the founders. Seeking to learn from the best, I joined Google's Assistant team, leading launches for new speech and camera features, including Continued Conversation and Face Match. This was my entry into AI product management, before the generative AI boom!

After five years and multiple successful launches, I transitioned to Google Labs, where I most recently led product development for the Gemini API and Google AI Studio for Developers. Now I'm focused on building new products with generative AI, embracing the thrill of 0-to-1. Part of what I love so much about 0-to-1 projects and the current AI space is working on difficult problems, figuring out whether something is even possible, and navigating around hard constraints on what's able to be built.

Describe a day in your life as an AI product leader.

Google I/O 2024, where I launched new features for the Gemini API and AI Studio onstage during the Developer Keynote, highlighted just how drastically the pace of AI has accelerated. What used to take months or even years—building, iterating, refining, optimizing—now happens in weeks. Comparing this year to 2019, when I launched Face Match, a more "traditional AI" feature, it's mind-blowing just how much faster things are moving right now.

This speed means constant learning is key. My typical day includes absorbing information from podcasts, research papers, articles, and more. I also dedicate time to strategic thinking and writing, crafting PRDs, strategy documents, and "thought pieces" to crystallize ideas. Of course, being a PM means meetings—though I aim for maximum efficiency—along with one-on-ones with my team and peers, often opting for "walk and talks." I also try to attend at least one tech event monthly to stay ahead of the curve and expose myself to how others are thinking about things.

Currently, my focus is split between managing a team of PMs and driving individual product work. This dual role ensures that I'm providing my team with clear direction, validating our road map, and clearing roadblocks, while also staying hands-on with the products we're building.

What do you want people coming into the field to know?
Here's what I want anyone entering the AI PM field to know: we are still in the incredibly early stages. The difference between you and someone with "years of experience" is likely a matter of months. You absolutely have time to catch up, and even get ahead.

Many of the core tenets of being a great PM still hold true: be relentlessly curious, embrace continuous learning, and deeply understand the problems you're solving.

That said, two things are especially crucial for aspiring AI PMs. First, embrace relentless learning. AI moves at warp speed, so what's "best" is constantly evolving. Stay updated on the latest advancements and their product implications. Second, develop a strong "product-level" understanding of AI by getting your hands dirty. Generative AI is powerful but requires a shift in thinking. It's not a magic bullet, and these models are probabilistic, not deterministic. Play with different tools, build something, and try integrating AI into your everyday life—recently I tried making a short film using AI, and I learned so much in the process! This hands-on experience is invaluable for understanding the technology's capabilities, limitations, and potential applications.

ARUN RAO

Arun Rao is GenAI product lead at Meta (Llama team).

What was your path to AI product management?
It was accidental. I was a quant derivatives trader at PIMCO [Investment Management] and wanted to spend all of my time on deep learning and building social robots. I founded a startup that pivoted from robotic pets to voice chat assistants for recommending financial products, and then shut it down as a profitable startup with not enough growth. I decided that PMing the products was my favorite part and then joined Amazon Music ML, and later came to Meta Ads Ranking and then GenAI.

Describe a day in your life as an AI product leader.
I have my plan for Monday through Wednesday, my top priorities. I have blocked out time for deep work and reading, and a chaotic mess of meetings around that to learn about needs from customers, partners, leadership, and others. I try to read between two and five AI papers a week, very efficiently, and this takes effort to keep the time for it. I'm constantly prioritizing which meetings to attend when I'm double- or triple-booked (whether I can add value, or if it's better if I touch base async to assist or give input).

Success in any week is pushing my three to five top priorities forward and being as useful as possible to others in a dozen or more areas. Often it's connecting where many needs overlap (the customers, the business, leadership requests, etc.), and learning how to gracefully defer or say no when needs can't be met. Ultimately, AI is just a path to build something great that people want—it constrains the method and solutions, but choosing the most important customer segments and their key problems is at the heart of PM work.

What do you want people coming into the field to know?

It's hard—I feel like AI PM is the neurosurgery of PM work. You have to learn a ton of specialized knowledge and keep up with a firehose of papers and research, while working with highly technical teams to implement ideas, where small mistakes can have big consequences.

NINO TASCA

Nino Tasca is chief product officer of Northstar Travel Group.

What was your path to AI product management?

I started out as a software engineer, but early in my career I realized that I had more passion for using technology to help solve user needs than for pushing technology for the sake of technology. While working as an engineer during the day, I went to NYU Stern [School of Business] at night and received my MBA. That credential proved to be an accelerant on my path to product management.

Describe a day in your life as an AI product leader.

As a product leader, the biggest focus should be on understanding customer needs, prioritization, and resource allocation. Once you reach a certain level of seniority in your career, your primary job is not always about figuring out the best solution. What is most important is understanding what the opportunities are, making sure you have the right team to capitalize on those opportunities, and then setting those people up for success.

What do you want people coming into the field to know?

AI is an amazing tool, but it is not a product in itself. With the increase in software possibilities with AI, the fundamentals of true product management become even more important. That's focusing on customer needs and making sure that you are bringing the right solutions to market. Users don't care about what technology is used. They care about which product meets their needs.

YANA WELINDER

Yana Welinder is the CEO and founder of Kraftful.

What was your path to AI product management?
I transitioned into product management after a diverse career in law, tech policy, and academia. As a professor, I authored the most cited paper on the policy implications of AI and computer vision, published in the Harvard Journal of Law and Technology. My research at Stanford and Harvard opened doors to speak at the White House, the UN Internet Governance Forum, and other intellectually stimulating events. Yet, I always felt something was missing in my work. Returning to industry as a Director at the Wikimedia Foundation, I had two significant opportunities to dive into product management: (1) leading the product, research, and design team to develop strategy recommendations for improving the Wikipedia readership experience; and (2) spearheading the transition of Wikipedia to encrypted access (HTTPS by default).

These experiences revealed what had been missing: the tangible, user-focused impact of building products. Next, I became PM number two at Carbon, a fast-growing unicorn disrupting manufacturing and enabling previously impossible designs—most notably the Adidas shoe with a lattice structure. This role was a crash course in product management, spanning software, hardware, and materials science, all supported by an in-house R&D lab. I worked on various AI-enabled products before founding Kraftful, where I now build AI products for product managers, combining my passions for product craft, AI, and innovation.

Describe a day in your life as a CEO of an AI startup.
Startups always operate in dog years, and AI capabilities are growing exponentially. Running an AI startup right now feels like sprinting at the speed of light—yet somehow never fast enough. I reflected on this yesterday while rebuilding our AI analysis with the latest large language models. This involves experimenting with new prompts and parameters of the latest large language models, work I usually tackle on weekends when I'm not in

meetings. During the week, I share my findings with our engineers, who then build the architecture to scale the prompt chain I've developed. This sparks frequent impromptu meetings to review results and fine-tune our approach.

At the same time, other engineers are focused on new features and UI improvements, where my role shifts to traditional product management—defining features and collaborating with design and engineering to bring them to life. A large part of my day is also spent talking with customers via calls or Intercom, gaining insights into how we can make Kraftful better. This is especially critical when building an AI product that has never existed before—our customers refine their requirements as they use it, helping us adapt and improve in real time.

What do you want someone who's coming into the field to know—one piece of advice if they're considering becoming an AI PM?

AI is a rapidly evolving field, and entering it can feel like merging onto a fast-moving freeway. The key is to stay up-to-date with the latest trends, models, and tools while mastering the fundamentals. Familiarize yourself with core concepts like machine learning, natural language processing, and neural networks. You don't need to be an AI engineer, but you should be comfortable discussing these technologies with your team. Your role is to translate complex AI capabilities into solutions that users find valuable and easy to adopt. Most importantly, focus on building a product that solves a real problem. Always start with the problem in mind—this will keep you from creating an AI solution in search of a problem.

MY TWO CENTS

Here are my two cents. First, don't get overwhelmed. There's a wealth of information, opinions, tutorials, and best practices out there, each shedding light on some aspect of AI. Be open to it all, stay curious, and make it your own. Also, figure out how AI can benefit your specific audience, based on your unique skills and perspective. Remember, AI is ultimately just a tool waiting for you to mold it in the best possible way to add value to users. Your journey in AI product leadership is about finding your own path. So, absorb knowledge, experiment, and discover how you can uniquely contribute to this exciting field. The future of AI is yours to shape.

If you're interested in learning more, I offer AI product management certifications via my AI PM Bootcamp (*https://marily.substack.com*) through the AI Product Academy.

CROSS-FUNCTIONAL COLLABORATION

As an AI PM, one of your most critical responsibilities is to lead cross-functional collaboration across a diverse array of stakeholders. The success of AI products, like any innovative technology, relies on a shared understanding and seamless coordination between teams. This section breaks down the key stakeholders you'll work with, focusing on their roles and contributions throughout the product lifecycle.

For a practical example, let's consider you're an AI PM at Amazon, leading a significant product update for Alexa, the company's smart assistant. Your goal is to enhance Alexa's ability to help users manage daily tasks at home. Who do you need to engage with to bring this vision to life? (Please note that smaller companies will have fewer cross-functional partners to deal with.)

AI and ML teams

Your first point of contact will be the AI team. The core of Alexa's value lies in its intelligent features—voice recognition, task management, and natural language understanding; elements built and refined by this team. ML scientists, red/blue teams, and MLOps personnel are your key allies here, tasked with developing and operationalizing the models that power your product:

- *ML scientists* focus on building the models that define Alexa's ability to understand and respond to commands. These experts will require large datasets to train their models—possibly sourced internally or acquired from third-party providers—and will iterate through various models until they achieve the right balance of performance and efficiency.

- *Red/blue teams* work on the security front, with the red teams conducting simulated attacks to expose vulnerabilities while the blue teams defend against these attacks. This helps ensure that your product remains robust in the face of real-world security threats. These teams play an essential role in making sure your AI is not just functional, but also secure.

- *MLOps teams* deploy the ML models the scientists create into a live environment. They focus on maintaining the infrastructure and processes that enable continuous integration and monitoring of these models, which is especially critical when scaling across a large customer base, such as Alexa's millions of users.

In short, your AI and ML teams bring the technical innovations to life, and you'll work closely with them to ensure that the models meet both the product vision and the users' needs.

Operations teams

The operations side of your collaboration involves teams that ensure the smooth running of all data pipelines, infrastructure, and project management aspects of the product lifecycle:

- *Program managers* coordinate efforts across different teams, ensuring that timelines, resource allocation, and the overall project scope align with business and technical objectives. They help you manage the project from a high level, navigating risks, dependencies, and bottlenecks to keep things on track.

- *Data operations (DataOps) teams* collect, clean, and integrate the data needed to train and deploy AI models. They ensure that your AI models are built on reliable, high-quality data while maintaining compliance with regulatory standards, such as GDPR. This collaboration is crucial, because the success of your product depends on the integrity and relevance of the data feeding your AI models.

Together, these teams lay the groundwork for efficient and compliant data handling, aligning operational capabilities with the AI-driven goals of the product.

Engineering teams

Engineers are the bridge between AI models and real-world applications, translating ML innovations into fully functional products. Great collaboration with engineering is vital for translating AI models into a seamless user experience. The technical integration between AI innovations and the product's real-world functionality requires close cooperation to ensure success:

- *Developers* are tasked with integrating AI models into the product's architecture. They need clear communication from AI PMs to implement the AI models' requirements effectively, ensuring that user interactions flow seamlessly within the application. Regular check-ins, code reviews, and technical discussions help ensure alignment and progress.

- *Testers* rigorously evaluate the functionality of the product, ensuring that the AI models work as intended in real-world scenarios. Their feedback helps AI PMs identify edge cases, potential bugs, and areas for improvement.

- *Data engineers* maintain the data infrastructure that supports your AI product. They work on ensuring efficient data pipelines that can handle both current and future data demands.

- *Technical program managers* (TPMs) oversee the coordination of all engineering tasks, from setting timelines to resource allocation. This role is critical in maintaining transparency and making sure all teams are aligned in their execution.

UX teams

UX is paramount, particularly when introducing AI products to a broad audience. The UX team ensures that the product is intuitive, accessible, and engaging for users:

- *User researchers* help you gather actionable insights into how users interact with your product, highlighting pain points and opportunities for improvement. Their findings inform your road map and product priorities, ensuring that every update addresses real user needs.

- *UX developers and designers* work closely with you to translate AI-driven functionality into an intuitive and visually appealing user interface. This collaboration typically starts with wireframes and prototypes, evolving into refined designs that align with the AI model's capabilities.

- *Content specialists* ensure that any language or instructional content in the product is clear and on-brand, making complex AI functionalities easily understandable for users.

Business teams

The business side of your product development involves working closely with product marketing managers (PMMs), sales teams, and partnership managers:

- *PMMs* define the product's value proposition and position it in the market. You'll collaborate with them on go-to-market strategies, crafting messaging that aligns with both the technical capabilities and user benefits of the product. (While go-to-market strategies are critical for the success of any AI product, they are beyond the scope of this book.)

- *Sales teams* provide feedback from direct customer interactions, offering insights into pain points and selling points. These teams help you refine the product based on real-world customer responses and guide you in creating compelling pitches that resonate with target users.

- *Partnership managers* work with external stakeholders to build strategic alliances that can enhance the product's market reach or capabilities. Collaborating with partners may involve integrating third-party technologies or codeveloping features to meet mutual goals.

Third-party stakeholders

External vendors, original equipment manufacturers (OEMs), and consultants may be involved in providing specialized technology or expertise for your AI product:

- *Vendors and OEMs* supply specialized components or services, contributing to the technical capabilities of the product. Your role here is to manage these relationships, ensuring quality and timeliness while balancing cost considerations.

- *Consultants and research institutions* bring advanced knowledge and innovation, particularly useful for navigating complex AI challenges or exploring cutting-edge technologies.

Governance, risk, and compliance (GRC) experts

Finally, your AI product must adhere to legal, privacy, and compliance requirements. Collaborating with legal teams, privacy experts, and compliance specialists is essential to ensure that your product is built responsibly and within regulatory frameworks:

- *Legal counsel* advises on intellectual property, contracts, and other legal matters.
- *Privacy experts* ensure that your product adheres to data protection regulations such as GDPR and the California Consumer Privacy Act (CCPA) (*https://oreil.ly/ccpa*).
- *Compliance specialists* oversee the product's adherence to industry standards and internal governance policies.

Your collaboration with GRC stakeholders ensures that your product is as responsible and secure as it is innovative.

Leadership teams

Finally, engaging with senior leadership, such as the C-suite and investors, is crucial for gaining support and securing the resources needed for your product's success. They provide strategic direction, funding, and oversight, ensuring that your product aligns with the broader company vision and objectives:

- *C-suite leaders* define the strategic goals and objectives for your AI product, ensuring alignment with broader business priorities.
- *Investors* provide the necessary financial backing and often challenge you to think critically about the product's market potential and ROI.

Regular reviews with leadership ensure that your product remains on track and aligned with the company's overall mission (see "Product Reviews: Getting Buy-in from Leadership" on page 132 for more about this).

Conclusion

The AI PM is at the center of it all. You are the glue connecting these diverse teams and stakeholders. By effectively orchestrating the efforts of each group, the AI PM ensures that the final product is not only technologically advanced but also market ready and compliant with all necessary standards. This role demands a broad vision and an eye for detail, making it one of the most exciting and demanding positions in today's tech industry.

Effective collaboration among all stakeholders is essential for building successful AI products. The AI PM is the central point of contact who steers the project toward a common goal.

In Chapter 5, we'll explore the crucial metrics that determine the success of an AI product. We'll dive into the key areas you must focus on during development and uncover strategies to help you excel in your role. Consider it your road map to understanding what matters when building and measuring AI products. We'll cover everything from KPIs and user engagement metrics to continuous improvement techniques. By the end of the chapter, you'll have a solid grasp of how to track, measure, and boost the performance of your AI initiatives, making your work compelling, impactful, and rewarding.

Now that you have a clearer picture of where you might fit in this ladder and of the scope of responsibilities associated with each level of your career, the next step is to explore how you will bring these AI products to life. This involves understanding the AI lifecycle, building a strategic road map, and ensuring that your product decisions align with both the user experience and business objectives. In the upcoming chapters, I'll dive deeper into the practical aspects of taking AI products from concept to market, navigating challenges, and driving impactful user experiences.

5

Strategic Thinking in AI

In my classes and seminars, I often hear questions like: How should I introduce AI into my product strategy? What can AI do to add value to users and grow my organization and company? Should I build in-house or buy off-the-shelf?

This chapter focuses on thinking strategically as an AI product leader and on the important decisions you might need to make.

Your Business Strategy: Evaluating AI As a Solution

Traditionally, only product leadership (group PMs, VPs, directors) would be involved in discussions on the strategic direction of a product area. However, what I have been observing nowadays with AI is that some strategic decisions are taking place even at the lowest level of a product manager's career, and it is crucial for all PMs, regardless of level, to involve leadership and seek feedback and input from them regularly while adopting AI. This company-wide conversation is even more vital when you're considering, for example, whether to build your AI capabilities in-house or outsource the job to external vendors. I will cover the build-versus-buy debate later in this chapter, but for now, know that having a cohesive AI strategy that permeates your company's culture is very important.

Let's assume for a second that you work for a company that already has an existing product offering with little to no AI, and you're confident that the organization does need AI. Your first step should be to research and answer the following questions:

- Map AI's capabilities to your company's mission. Can AI contribute to your company's goals? How can it solve existing problems? How might it augment the current user experience or streamline operations?

- Identify key pain points in your existing product offering(s) to solve. Where might AI make a significant difference for a specific user segment of your current product(s)? Examples might be improving personalization, automating routine tasks, or offering predictive analytics to enhance decision making.

- Estimate the impact on users. How will adding AI affect your user base? Will it improve their experience or make the product more accessible? Will it enhance the core KPIs you and the company care about?

- Introducing AI might solve some problems, but it could also introduce new complexities. What are the benefits of integrating AI? What are the potential downsides (such as increased development costs or longer time to market)? How much importance do you attach to each of these benefits and downsides? When you weigh them against one another, what is the result?

- AI features need constant optimization and maintenance. Can your company sustain the long-term upkeep of any AI-driven features you choose to integrate? Does the company have the resources in place that it will need to provide continued support for the AI-driven product, including talent, expertise, and infrastructure?

- How are your competitors using AI? Is there a competitive edge involved in adopting AI in your product? How does the market landscape influence the urgency and approach of your AI integration?

In the Appendix, you can find a worksheet designed to help you with this process.

AI MIGHT NOT ALWAYS BE THE ANSWER

The decisions you make around AI are never straightforward. They require balancing the company's immediate business needs with its long-term strategic goals. For instance, should you develop in-house AI capabilities, which might take longer but offers more control and customization? Or should you purchase third-party solutions to get to market faster, with the trade-off being less flexibility?

Every decision in your business strategy must consider internal factors such as available talent, infrastructure, and expertise, as well as external factors such as market trends and competition. You also need to identify your short-term and long-term AI strategies to ensure that your AI initiatives are suited to your company's broader strategic objectives.

Adding AI just for the sake of adding AI is a common mistake. By the time you know what problem your AI solution is intended to solve, you should be well aware that not every problem requires an AI solution. Incorporating AI into a product without a thoughtful AI strategy is a recipe for disaster. When you're considering integrating AI into a business process or product, make sure there's a clear reason—and a problem that *only* AI can solve.

While AI has the potential to solve a wide range of problems, it's important to recognize that it isn't always the right tool for the job. In some cases, using AI may introduce unnecessary complexity, costs, or risks. Here are some scenarios where AI might not be the best solution:

Don't use AI when there is another way to solve the problem.
  Chances are good that alternative solutions will have less risk, cost less, and lead to equally good outcomes. Before diving into AI, consider whether simpler approaches could achieve the same result. Can you solve the problem more quickly and at a lower cost without AI? Sometimes the answer is yes, and that's OK. For example, basic automation scripts or rule-based systems might be sufficient for certain tasks. Always evaluate the problem space thoroughly to ensure that AI *really is* the most effective method to pursue.

Don't use AI if you can't get good data.
  Data is the heart of AI. Having enough high-quality data is crucial for training effective AI models. If obtaining quality data is a struggle from the start and ends up being impossible, AI might not be the best path forward. Not every use case can provide the volume, diversity, and quality of data necessary for AI to work reliably. In these situations, consider alternatives that do not rely heavily on data, such as deterministic logic or simpler statistical methods. (See "Your Data Strategy: Populating and Adapting Your Model" on page 129 for more.)

Don't use AI if you're not ready for the challenges of productionizing it.

Building an AI prototype is easy, but productionizing AI is not. Many organizations underestimate the challenges involved in deploying and maintaining AI systems in real-world environments. If AI is in its infancy in your organization, you need a compelling reason to go down this path. Robust production requires significant infrastructure investment to support scalability, security, latency, and continuous monitoring—factors that add significant overhead to your AI initiative. Additionally, consider your current tech stack: some companies acquire smaller startups with great technology, but later have to rewrite all of their code due to incompatibilities. This is a critical factor to assess early on.

Don't use AI if you're worried it will cost too much.

AI solutions can be expensive to build, deploy, and maintain. From hiring data scientists to securing computational resources, the costs can quickly add up. Before moving forward, ask yourself if outsourcing AI development would strain your organization's budget. Also, weigh these costs against the potential benefits to determine if AI offers a justifiable return on investment. Sometimes a simpler, less costly solution can address the problem adequately.

Don't use AI if you aren't prepared to maintain and iterate on your solution indefinitely.

Do you have the data, infrastructure, and models you need to develop and maintain an AI solution? Remember that the work doesn't stop once you train and launch a model. Ongoing maintenance is essential, so you'll need to plan for it.

In short, although AI is a powerful tool, it's not always the answer. While there are no definitive right or wrong answers, these questions will help guide you toward the best path forward. After addressing them, the key is to determine whether the problem is significant enough to warrant the investment of time and resources.

Equally important is evaluating the associated costs and trade-offs. As discussed in Chapter 3, trade-offs aren't about simply choosing between A and B; instead, think of them as sliders that need careful adjustment. By exploring and balancing the interactions between multiple factors, you can tailor your approach to achieve the optimal outcome.

DISRUPTIVE OR SUSTAINING? NAVIGATING THE INNOVATOR'S DILEMMA

Once you've identified how AI can be integrated into your product to solve a problem or create a new offering, it's time to consider whether your AI solution is disruptive or sustaining. This is a critical strategic question, and understanding where your AI product fits can have a huge impact on the direction your company takes. Every innovative company faces this challenge, best known as the "Innovator's Dilemma," a concept Harvard Business School professor Clayton Christensen introduced in his book *The Innovator's Dilemma* (Harvard Business Review Press, 1997). In the book, Christensen explores how successful companies, despite doing everything right, can still fail when faced with "disruptive technologies," pointing out that the strategies that led to a company's current dominance may become ineffective when new technologies and innovative approaches emerge, threatening to change the status quo.

The dilemma presents two types of innovation. A *sustaining* innovation improves upon existing products to better meet customer needs. It's typically incremental—improving performance, reducing defects, or enhancing user experience—and it aligns with the company's current strategy. For example, adding AI-driven predictive analytics to an existing product to offer better personalization might fall under sustaining innovation. The key here is that sustaining innovations meet your customers' *current* needs.

By contrast, a *disruptive* innovation introduces a product or solution that initially targets niche markets or unmet needs in a way that may seem inferior to the current offerings. These innovations often appear less powerful, less refined, or less desirable to the mainstream market. However, they address a niche need so effectively that they eventually redefine the market. Disruptive innovations meet your customers' *future* needs, potentially creating new markets or reshaping entire industries.

Take the camera market, for example. Before the rise of smartphones, point-and-shoot cameras were the go-to option for anyone who wanted to take high-quality digital photos. But smartphones disrupted that market. Early on, smartphone cameras didn't match the quality of point-and-shoot options, but they were *good enough* for most people and offered the added convenience of always being at hand. What was once a niche offering (phone cameras) quickly became the dominant product. Despite being "inferior" in quality at first, smartphones met the evolving needs of users—portability and convenience—eventually leading to the decline of standalone camera markets.

What would a sustaining innovation for the camera market have been? Perhaps improving point-and-shoot features like megapixel count or autofocus speed—enhancements that serve existing users but don't fundamentally change the nature of the product or market. Now consider how this applies to AI product development. The decision between pursuing a sustaining AI innovation and pursuing a disruptive one is crucial. Sustaining AI solutions may involve integrating existing AI technologies to improve current offerings—such as automating routine processes or improving customer service chatbots. These AI-driven improvements align with what your product already offers and are designed to help you stay competitive within your current market.

On the other hand, disruptive AI innovations might challenge the way your company has traditionally solved problems. Perhaps you're using AI to create an entirely new product category that targets an unmet need, even if it seems to offer less functionality or appeal at first glance. The risk is greater, but so is the potential reward, if you can carve out new opportunities in niche markets.

Disruptive innovations tend to begin with lower performance in the areas that traditional customers value. They might not have the polish, reliability, or robust feature set that mature products possess. This makes it difficult for larger companies, especially those serving demanding clients, to justify investing in these nascent technologies. After all, why would a company move forward with a new AI-driven product if it doesn't immediately match the features of its existing, proven offerings?

However, disruptive innovations succeed because they *prioritize different performance metrics*. Rather than focusing on current users, they target new or underserved segments. Over time, these innovations evolve, and as they improve, they often surpass traditional products in ways that redefine the market.

Your AI Strategy: To Build or to Buy?

One of the most frequent and critical questions that arise when adopting AI is whether to build an in-house AI solution or buy one from a third-party vendor. Both approaches come with distinct advantages and challenges. I'll break down the key benefits of each approach and guide you through the decision-making process.

First, let's look at the advantages of building your own AI model in-house:

Customization

Building AI in-house allows you to tailor the solution precisely to your product's requirements. This ensures a solution that can evolve as your business scales and pivots. Custom models, built from the ground up, can be tailored to handle highly specific tasks but require more data and resources. They are suitable for highly specialized tasks for which a pretrained model's performance might fall short. Custom models provide more flexibility but require significant data, compute resources, and expertise.

Ownership

Full ownership over the technology means that you control both the data and the AI model. This is particularly valuable in industries where proprietary data and differentiation are key to gaining a competitive edge.

Data security

Keeping data in-house reduces the risk of breaches and allows for greater control over compliance with data privacy regulations such as GDPR and HIPAA.

Long-term cost savings

While the initial costs of developing an in-house AI system are higher, the long-term savings may outweigh these up-front expenses. Once developed, there are no ongoing licensing or subscription fees.

There are also advantages to buying a pretrained AI solution:

Faster time to market

A pretrained model or third-party solution allows you to integrate AI into your product more quickly. This can be a key competitive advantage in fast-moving markets. Pretrained models offer a head start, providing general capabilities that can be fine-tuned for specific applications.

Access to expertise

Buying from established vendors gives you access to specialized AI knowledge and models that have been tested across multiple use cases and industries, ensuring reliability. Pretrained models are ideal when you want to leverage existing general AI capabilities, especially in domains such as NLP and image recognition.

Scalability

Many pretrained AI solutions are built with scalability in mind, which means they can easily handle growing datasets and increased traffic without requiring significant rework.

Continuous updates and support

AI evolves rapidly, and with a third-party solution, you can benefit from continuous updates and improvements. This ensures that your system remains up-to-date with minimal effort on your part.

Now that you know the advantages of each approach, deciding whether to build an in-house AI solution or buy a pretrained AI model comes down to your broader AI strategy and the specific context of your business. Here are the key factors to consider when making this important decision:

Core competency

If AI is core to your product's value proposition, building in-house allows you to fully customize and control the solution, offering a better alignment with your business needs. This can enhance the overall user experience and scalability. However, if AI is only a supporting feature, buying a third-party solution can help you quickly integrate the necessary functionality at a lower cost.

Resources and expertise

Building AI in-house requires significant investment in talent, including data scientists and ML engineers, as well as infrastructure such as data storage and compute power. If your organization has the resources and the long-term commitment needed to build AI internally, this option may deliver a tailored solution. On the other hand, if your company lacks the expertise or infrastructure, buying from a third-party provider is a viable option. Third-party vendors bring with them specialized knowledge and have already invested in the talent and infrastructure necessary for AI development.

Time to market

Developing custom AI solutions can be time-consuming, which may delay your product's launch. If speed is a priority, buying pretrained AI models allows for faster deployment and enables your company to stay competitive in fast-moving markets. This is especially critical in industries where being first to market offers a significant advantage.

Long-term strategy

When AI plays a crucial role in your long-term strategy, building in-house can provide more flexibility and control in the future. Custom-built AI solutions allow your company to pivot or evolve its AI capabilities as needed. However, for short-term solutions or when AI is not a long-term focus, purchasing a pretrained model can fulfill immediate needs without the resource-heavy investment required for in-house development.

Cost

Building AI internally requires up-front investments in infrastructure, talent, and time but could offer long-term savings by avoiding licensing fees. Purchasing a pretrained AI model can reduce initial expenses and time to market, although recurring licensing or usage fees can accumulate over time, impacting the total cost of ownership.

Uncertainty is also a big factor in this decision, as you'll recall from Chapter 1, where we discussed the probabilistic nature of AI. AI comes with its own set of risks, particularly in areas like algorithmic failures, scalability issues, and responsible AI practices. For example, Tesla's Autopilot AI has faced scrutiny due to accidents in real-world environments, highlighting the risks involved in deploying AI in critical applications. Purchased AI solutions may alleviate some of these risks by offering tried-and-tested models, but they also make you dependent on external vendors for updates, fixes, and continued support.

Last, it's always a good idea to research what your competitors are doing. For example, in 2019 Salesforce acquired Tableau, a leading data visualization company, to quickly enhance its analytics capabilities and compete more effectively with rivals. Building a comparable solution in-house would have taken Salesforce significantly longer, potentially causing the company to lose ground to competitors like SAP and Oracle.

THE BUILD-VERSUS-BUY DECISION MATRIX

Taking the preceding factors into account, I've created a matrix (Table 5-1) that helps me visualize and summarize when making this type of decision.

Table 5-1. The build-versus-buy decision matrix

Factor	Build in-house	Buy pretrained
Core competency	Ideal if AI is core to the product's value proposition, offering customization and control	Best if AI is a secondary feature, providing quicker implementation at a lower cost
Resources and expertise	Requires investment in data scientists, ML engineers, and infrastructure	Ideal if your company lacks AI expertise and infrastructure
Time to market	Takes longer to develop, which may delay product launches	Fastest option for deployment, allowing for rapid market entry
Long-term strategy	Offers greater flexibility and control for future needs	Suitable for short-term solutions or interim AI needs
Cost assessment	High up-front costs, but potential long-term savings by avoiding licensing fees	Lower initial costs, but recurring expenses may add up over time
Risk and uncertainty	Higher risks, particularly for critical applications; requires internal management of risks	Mitigates some risks, but makes you dependent on external vendors for updates and fixes
Data privacy and ethics	Ensures stricter control over sensitive data, reducing privacy risks	May introduce privacy concerns if data is shared with a third-party vendor
Competitive landscape	Slower, but allows for more control over competitive differentiators	Enables rapid response to competition, but may offer less differentiation over time

The decision you make should align with your company's core competencies, available resources, and strategic objectives. In some cases, a hybrid approach—leveraging third-party AI solutions for certain functionalities while developing proprietary AI in-house for others—can be the most effective strategy. We'll discuss that option next.

HYBRID APPROACHES: A BALANCED STRATEGY

In a hybrid approach, you might choose to build core AI components in-house while leveraging third-party solutions for nonessential or supplementary capabilities. For example, you could build your proprietary recommendation engine in-house, but use a pretrained language model like GPT-3 for NLP tasks. Another example might be a music streaming service, where you could initially use a pretrained LLM to understand song lyrics and generate metadata. However, if your aim is to develop a unique model that identifies and classifies niche musical genres, building a custom model might be more effective.

For example, OpenAI's GPT-4 model, available via API, allows businesses to integrate advanced natural language understanding capabilities into their products without extensive development time. This highlights how pretrained models can speed up your time to market. Tesla's Autopilot driving feature, however, has shown both the benefits and the risks of building AI in-house. While it allows Tesla to innovate rapidly, it also highlights the need for thorough risk management in critical applications such as autonomous driving.

Assuming that you want to move forward with in-house AI development, you need to have a good data and model strategy in place. Let's take a look at that next.

Your Data Strategy: Populating and Adapting Your Model

As you learned in Chapter 2, data is the backbone of AI. However, depending on the product and use case, acquiring high-quality, labeled, real-world data can be challenging. In such cases, using *synthetic data*—artificially generated data that simulates real-world scenarios—becomes a viable option. It's also important to recognize that the choice of algorithms and learning methods is only part of the equation. Equally crucial is deciding how to adapt these models to meet your product's unique needs. This section discusses both of these data decisions.

SYNTHETIC VERSUS REAL-WORLD DATA

Let's talk about synthetic data. It's a tool that can be incredibly powerful when used correctly, but it's not a silver bullet. Think about it as functioning for AI like a flight simulator functions for pilots. Before getting into a real plane, pilots spend countless hours in simulators that create synthetic scenarios they might encounter in the real world. The same principle applies to AI.

In general, I have seen synthetic data work wonders in healthcare. I first generated synthetic data during my PhD research (*https://oreil.ly/o9HiZ*), when I needed data from influenza outbreaks to try to predict when an infection would die down. Companies like Syntegra (*https://oreil.ly/oazJT*) are creating incredibly realistic (but fake) medical records and images that let AI models learn without compromising anyone's privacy. Self-driving car companies use synthetic data too: Waymo's virtual testing environment, called SimulationCity (*https://oreil.ly/i6t33*), lets the company test its vehicles in millions of synthetic scenarios. It's much safer and more efficient than trying to encounter every possible road situation in real life.

But here's the thing—synthetic data has its limits. If you're building a recommendation engine for your ecommerce site, there's no substitute for real user behavior. You can generate synthetic shopping patterns all day long, but they won't capture the subtle nuances of how real people browse, compare, and make purchasing decisions. The same goes for NLP. Synthetic conversations often miss the messy, wonderful complexity of how people actually communicate.

The key lies in knowing when to use which type of data. Here's what I've learned from working with various AI products:

Use synthetic data when . . .

- You're dealing with sensitive information (as in healthcare or financial services).

- You need to test rare but critical scenarios (such as accidents for self-driving cars).

- You're in early development and need to move fast.

- Real data collection could be prohibitively expensive.

Stick to real data when . . .

- User behavior and preferences are central to your product.

- You need to capture cultural or contextual nuances.

- You're making high-stakes decisions that directly affect users.

In some cases, the best approach might be a hybrid one. Start with synthetic data to get your models up and running, then gradually incorporate real data as you gather it. This is exactly what Tesla does (*https://oreil.ly/9jDIb*): it uses both synthetic scenarios and real-world driving data to train its autonomous driving systems.

Generating good synthetic data is an art in itself. The data needs to maintain the statistical properties of real data while avoiding any accidental patterns that could bias your model. Always validate your synthetic data against real samples when possible, and keep checking that your model's performance holds up in real-world conditions.

FINE-TUNING, RAG, OR GROUNDING?

Fine-tuning, retrieval-augmented generation (RAG), and grounding methods intersect with multiple learning techniques and are essential in determining how your AI model will function, integrate with existing data, and enhance user experiences. Several factors come into play, including latency, data availability, accuracy requirements, and scalability. Here's a more detailed look at each option, along with real-world AI product examples.

Fine-tuning

Fine-tuning involves taking a pretrained model and training it further on a specific dataset tailored to the problem at hand. It's most useful when your model needs to adapt its understanding based on new data to specialize in a particular task or domain. It's best used for scenarios where the accuracy of the model is paramount and the task is well-defined. Fine-tuning is resource intensive: it requires substantial labeled data and computational power.

Content moderation tools, like those used by social media platforms such as Facebook, are often fine-tuned to specialize in detecting hate speech or inappropriate content. The investment in fine-tuning is justified by the need for high precision and minimal errors. As another example, an audio streaming service might use fine-tuning to generate better personalized recommendations, training the model on user-specific listening behaviors to predict what songs a user is likely to enjoy.

RAG

RAG enhances generative models by incorporating a retrieval mechanism that accesses a large corpus of information. It provides up-to-date information dynamically, without requiring the model itself to be fully retrained. It's best used for dynamic, information-heavy contexts in which the model needs to access specific information that is not directly encoded in its parameters.

RAG is particularly effective for use cases in which information changes frequently, such as news or market trends. To continue our example, a music streaming service might use RAG to recommend music or podcasts that align with current social media trends or recent news about artists, offering real-time relevance. For instance, if a particular song becomes popular on TikTok, RAG could retrieve this information and use it to tailor recommendations quickly.

Grounding

Grounding uses preexisting context, usually via prompt engineering, to guide a base model's behavior. It's a more lightweight approach, adding instructions or context to influence the model's responses or predictions. I have seen it used when rapid iterations are needed and the model requires only slight adjustments or context to perform effectively.

This approach is less resource intensive than fine-tuning and does not require large datasets. For instance, in a customer support chatbot like those used by ecommerce platforms, you could implement grounding by prompting the model to adopt a particular tone, focus on specific information, or follow a predefined conversation flow. This can be especially useful during product experimentation, where changes need to be made quickly without retraining the model.

A decision-making framework for fine-tuning, RAG, and grounding

Choosing the right method depends on various factors, such as latency, data requirements, accuracy needs, and scalability. You can use Table 5-2 to help you decide which method is best for your use case.

Table 5-2. Factors to consider for fine-tuning, RAG, and grounding

Factor	Fine-tuning	RAG	Grounding
Latency	Higher latency due to deep processing	Can be optimized with fast retrieval	Low latency, uses preexisting context
Data needs	Requires large, labeled datasets	Requires a large corpus for retrieval	Minimal new data, relies on context
Accuracy	High; ideal for precision tasks	Variable; depends on retrieved data	Moderate; enhances context relevance
Scalability	Resource intensive	Scales with data corpus size	Easily scales with pretrained models

Product Reviews: Getting Buy-in from Leadership

Product reviews are essential checkpoints that help product teams get buy-in from leadership, ensure alignment, evaluate progress, and make strategic decisions. They provide an opportunity to engage stakeholders, present trade-offs, and gain feedback. In your AI product journey, you'll likely lead product reviews that involve presenting progress, gathering input, and making key decisions.

These reviews are usually performed by a steering committee made up of product and engineering leadership. It's a good practice (but optional) for the presenter or PM to add all cross-functional partners who might be affected by a specific upcoming launch.

There are several kinds of product reviews. Table 5-3 provides an overview.

Table 5-3. Key product review formats and their objectives

Review type	Objective	Key elements	Outcome
Decision review	Go/no-go decision, strategic direction	Present clear options with pros and cons, trade-offs, justifications	Clear decision with action items/next steps
Discussion review	Open-ended brainstorming, early-stage feedback	Encourage diverse opinions, focus on research and early insights	Gather feedback, refine product direction
Alignment review	Cross-functional alignment on vision, goals, timeline	Present vision and key milestones, surface any misalignments	Alignment with clear next steps
Status update	Progress report, milestones, challenges	Present KPIs, highlight roadblocks, offer transparency on risks	Keep stakeholders informed and aligned on progress

Here is a checklist for a great product review.

Before the review:

☐ Have you compiled all relevant information and key data points, including KPIs, milestones, user research, and market analysis, so that you can present a cohesive picture of where the product stands?

☐ Have you invited the right set of cross-functional partners?

☐ Have you shared the PRD or slide deck with all attendees beforehand so that participants come prepared and informed?

During the review:

☐ Are you clear on what you want to achieve from the review—a go/no-go decision, resource allocation, or alignment on a strategy? Does everyone understand the goal(s) of this product review?

☐ Are you encouraging a collaborative discussion with input from all key stakeholders, while keeping the conversation anchored to the review's objectives?

☐ Have you laid out the trade-offs, highlighting the risks, costs, benefits, and potential impact of different decisions?

After the review:

☐ Have you sent all attendees a summary with key decisions, next steps, and clear ownership of action items?

☐ Do you have a plan to monitor progress on the agreed-upon actions (e.g., holding a follow-up review, adding specific sections to the PRD, or gathering more data)?

Conclusion

This chapter explored the critical aspects of strategy in AI products. Introducing AI into your product strategy isn't just about following trends—it's about solving specific problems that align with your company's goals and user needs. Crafting an AI strategy requires careful consideration of various factors, such as deciding whether to build or buy an AI model, navigating the Innovator's Dilemma, and understanding complex trade-offs.

6

Setting Goals and Measuring Success

Unpacking success in AI products can be surprisingly challenging. No single metric can fully capture an AI product's impact. Instead, an understanding of success emerges from a balanced combination of diverse metrics working together to provide a comprehensive view of product health. When determining whether a product or feature is ready for launch, it's crucial to consider these metrics strategically. Remember, there's no one-size-fits-all recipe; the right metrics depend on the nature of your product, its users, and the problem it aims to solve.

To truly understand the performance of an AI feature, relying on a single metric will almost always fall short. The real insights come from examining multiple metrics in tandem. I like to think of this as an AI *product metric blend* (see Figure 6-1). Each metric highlights a specific aspect of the product's characteristics. By blending these metrics and examining the results, you can gain a holistic understanding of an AI feature's performance and overall impact.

A successful AI product has three core components: product health metrics, system health metrics, and AI proxy metrics. This chapter explores each in detail to build a solid foundation for evaluating your AI product's success, then presents a framework to help you craft the right OKRs.

Figure 6-1. *The product metric blend (source: Dr. Marily Nika)*

Product Health Metrics

Product health metrics, such as engagement, retention, and satisfaction, fall squarely within your domain of responsibility as an AI PM. These metrics will become the cornerstone of how you monitor and optimize your product.

Note

The lists in this and the following two sections are not comprehensive. Rather, they highlight the most commonly used product health metrics a PM may come across.

Let's break down the key metrics in this category by exploring an example that mirrors what you might encounter in your day-to-day work. Suppose you're the product manager for a (fictional) AI-driven fitness app that we'll call FitAI, which aims to become the go-to solution for fitness enthusiasts. Your mission? Continuously monitor and optimize FitAI using a variety of product health metrics:

Engagement

Engagement measures how actively users interact with your AI product. Frequency of use, session duration, and the number of interactions per session are strong indicators of engagement. For AI products, engagement often focuses on how frequently users rely on AI-driven features, such as recommendations or insights.

Imagine your users opening the FitAI app every morning to check out their personalized, AI-generated workout plans, track their progress, and share their achievements. High engagement here means the product is providing clear value. You can track this by measuring usage frequency, consistency, and time spent within the app. For example, you might experiment by introducing a new feature that allows users to adjust their workout intensity based on daily performance. An increase in engagement following the introduction of this feature could indicate it resonates with users, whereas a decrease might signal areas for improvement.

User satisfaction

While engagement is essential, it's usually closely linked with user satisfaction. This qualitative metric reflects how happy users are with your AI product. High satisfaction often translates into loyalty and advocacy. Surveys, feedback forms, and Net Promoter Scores (NPSs) (*https://oreil.ly/ E7dFZ*) are great ways to measure this. For AI products, satisfaction also hinges on whether the AI meets user expectations, provides relevant outputs, and enhances the overall experience.

In the context of FitAI, you may run surveys to discover that users are thrilled with the app's personalized workout plans and progress tracking but find the interface rigid and unfriendly. This feedback can guide you in making design decisions that make the app more intuitive, directly impacting user satisfaction scores.

Adoption

Adoption tracks the rate at which new users start using your AI product. High adoption suggests that the product is gaining traction in the market. Monitoring sign-up rates and identifying trends can provide insights into what drives user adoption, like successful marketing campaigns or word of mouth.

Suppose FitAI experiences a surge in new users after a partnership with a famous sports team, like the Boston Celtics. This spike in adoption confirms that the product is on the right track, encouraging you to explore additional collaborations to sustain growth.

Conversion

Conversion measures to what extent you've achieved your end goal. For example, sales bots and agents should be measured on their ability to close deals. A donation solicitation bot should be measured on the number of donations received after engagement.

Retention

Retention rates measure how well your AI product keeps users coming back over time. This is the metric that tests your product's lasting value. For FitAI, retention would be counted when users not only download the app but also consistently use it to meet their fitness goals.

Suppose you notice that users who complete their first AI-recommended workout are 50% more likely to remain active. This insight suggests that new features should focus on guiding users through their initial interactions, possibly with gamified rewards, to boost retention. It is also important to measure churn. *Churn* is the flip side of retention. It's the rate at which users stop using your product. Analyzing churn patterns can provide valuable insights into potential issues. If you notice a wave of users quitting FitAI after one month because they find the AI-generated workouts repetitive, it signals an opportunity to introduce customizable workout options. Understanding why users leave is just as crucial as knowing why they stay.

Financial metrics

Financial metrics such as revenue and ROI gauge the economic impact of your product. For FitAI, assessing the balance between costs and revenue from subscriptions and in-app purchases will help you make informed decisions about future investments.

Your job as an AI PM is to monitor these product health metrics continuously, analyze them, and implement strategies for optimization. This often means collaborating with your development team to address technical issues and adjusting your marketing strategies to boost adoption and retention. Now let's pivot to system health metrics to understand how the product performs under the hood.

System Health Metrics

While your main focus as an AI PM might be on product health, it's essential to have a grasp of system health metrics. These metrics reveal how the product performs at a technical level, providing insights into scalability, reliability, and overall performance. They include factors such as the following:

Uptime and latency
Uptime tracks how often the system is available to users, while latency measures the system's response time. High uptime and low latency are vital for maintaining user trust. For FitAI, maximizing uptime and minimizing latency ensures a smooth experience as users interact with their personalized workout plans.

Scalability
Scalability becomes critical as your user base grows. By conducting load testing and monitoring resource usage during peak traffic, you can ensure that your AI system can handle increasing loads effectively.

Error rate
Error rates track the frequency of system errors. High error rates can lead to user dissatisfaction and disengagement. If FitAI experiences a spike in errors after a new feature release, it's a prompt to investigate and resolve bugs swiftly.

To maintain system health, routine monitoring and audits are essential. Implement automated alerts for key metrics and conduct stress tests regularly. Developing an incident response plan will help you act swiftly if issues arise.

With system health under control, let's now focus on the AI component—the proxy metrics that directly impact model performance.

AI Proxy Metrics

Similarly to system health metrics, you may not have direct control over AI proxy metrics as an AI PM. Still, you must recognize when these metrics indicate a change in how the user base interacts with a product. AI proxy metrics play a pivotal role in assessing trade-offs and making strategic decisions, and they serve as a yardstick for evaluating the effectiveness of the underlying model. Proxy metrics focus on the integrity of the underlying models used in a product.

In ML, proxy metrics play a significant role in gauging model accuracy. The name *proxy* reflects that they measure the model's performance but are different from the ultimate goal of the product or feature. Let me give you a few examples.

MODEL QUALITY METRICS

Model quality refers to the effectiveness of a trained model in making predictions or decisions based on new, unseen data. It is typically assessed through various performance metrics that indicate how well the model's predictions align with actual outcomes.

Understanding model quality is crucial for AI PMs because it directly impacts the reliability, efficiency, and impact of an AI product. For instance, in a healthcare AI application used to diagnose diseases, high precision ensures that the diagnoses provided by the model are correct. In contrast, high recall ensures that the model identifies as many true cases of the disease as possible. Poor model quality could lead to incorrect diagnoses, potentially harming patients and damaging the credibility of the healthcare provider.

As an AI PM, you must critically evaluate model performance using these metrics to manage AI products effectively. This involves understanding what each metric tells you about the model's behavior and how to improve these metrics through various optimization strategies.

The AIPDL, which we've explored throughout this book, is inherently iterative. After deployment, you'll frequently revisit earlier phases, particularly model training and validation, as new user data becomes available. This iterative cycle includes a series of experiments where you run evaluations (evals) to compare the performance of the live model against offline versions. These evaluations help you determine if a new model offers a significant improvement, guiding your decision on whether it's time to launch the updated version.

Let's cover a few of the most frequently used model quality metrics, using the example of a system that classifies incoming emails by whether or not they are spam:

Accuracy

We measure the accuracy of this email classification feature by the percentage of correct classifications made by the system. Think of it as a test; out of all the emails classified, how many did the algorithm accurately identify as spam or nonspam?

Precision

Precision is the ratio of true positive results to all positive results predicted by the model. It determines the accuracy of positive predictions. In our spam example, out of all the emails the algorithm marked as spam, we want to know the number of emails that are truly spam. High precision indicates that the model has few false positives; in other words, fewer type I errors.

Sensitivity

Sensitivity measures how good the model is at finding all the positive cases. Let's use the spam example to provide some context. The sensitivity metric evaluates the algorithm's success in identifying every spam email in our inbox. High sensitivity means you have few false negatives—in other words, fewer type II errors.

Recall

Recall measures the model's ability to correctly identify all relevant positive cases. In the spam example, it tells us how many of the actual spam emails were successfully flagged by the algorithm. High recall indicates that the model misses very few spam emails, meaning it is effective at capturing positive cases with minimal false negatives. Suppose there are 100 actual spam emails in the inbox, and the algorithm correctly identifies 80 of them as spam; however, it misses 20 spam emails by classifying them as nonspam. If the algorithm successfully identified 80% of all spam emails, you would say that it had 80% recall.

Receiver operating characteristic (ROC) curve

The ROC curve is a graphical representation that illustrates the trade-off between the true positive rate and the false positive rate at various threshold settings. In the context of our spam example, the ROC curve helps evaluate how well the model can distinguish between spam and nonspam emails across different decision thresholds. A model with a curve closer to the top-left corner has better discriminatory power.

OBJECTIVE FUNCTIONS

Objective functions are proxy metrics that evaluate an ML model's performance during training. They measure how well the model's predictions match the actual outcomes, guiding the learning process.

The most commonly used objective functions are *loss functions*, which calculate the difference between the predicted and actual values for each prediction. The goal is to minimize this loss to improve the model's accuracy. *Mean square error* (MSE), for example, is a loss function used for tasks that use regression models, called *regression tasks*. An example of a regression task is predicting the demand a store may experience for a given product. Depending on a set of features such as price or utility, a regression model can help predict the demand for the product.

MSE calculates the average of the squared differences between predicted and actual values. Imagine you are tasked with predicting the weekly sales of a new AI product in a popular retail store. Accurate sales predictions help you manage inventory effectively, cutting the losses from overstocking and stockouts. Suppose you predicted sales for Week 1 to be 100 units, but it was 50. The error for Week 1 is 50 units. Each week represents a "loss." The bigger the error, the higher the loss.

Now, imagine this happening over several weeks. The error differs each week, and you want to penalize weeks with a more significant error. To do this, you square the error. To get a meaningful metric across time, you then calculate the average of the squared errors and the MSE. Loss functions show how accurate a model's predictions are. Workshopping an algorithm to minimize loss functions will enable systems to work as intended.

When you're launching a feature or product, you aim to address specific user pain points. Just relying on an ML model is not sufficient. As a PM, you must ensure that your ML model is seamlessly integrated into a product experience so that users can benefit from the technology. Consider, for instance, a recommendation widget on Spotify that suggests new songs to enrich playlists, or a smart-matching feature on Tinder that connects individuals based on shared hobbies. Fusing the model with the user experience is the key to unlocking the true potential of this AI technology. By considering all of the metrics, you will get a complete picture of your AI feature's success.

CONFUSION MATRICES

Confusion matrices are handy evaluation tools highlighting many critical model performance metrics. A *confusion matrix* is a table of actual and predicted binary features used to evaluate a classification algorithm's performance. It provides a summary of prediction results on a classification problem. The matrix in Table 6-1 compares the actual values with the values predicted by the model.

Table 6-1. Describing the four elements of the confusion matrix for the email classification example

Type	Definition
True positive	When a prediction is correctly classified as spam
True negative	When a prediction is correctly classified as nonspam
False positive	When a prediction is incorrectly classified as spam
False negative	When a prediction is incorrectly classified as nonspam

This can be applied to a feature that distinguishes between spam and non-spam emails in your inbox, as shown in Figure 6-2.

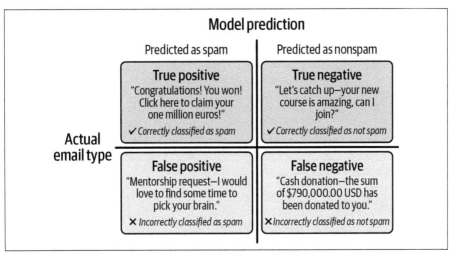

Figure 6-2. Visual representation of four possible outcomes when AI classifies emails as spam or nonspam

Figure 6-3 provides a visual representation of how the actual values and the values predicted by the model translate to the user experience.

Figure 6-3. AI proxy metrics inbox (source: Dr. Marily Nika)

OKRs for AI Products

Now that we've explored various metrics, it's time to discuss how these metrics can transform into actionable OKRs. The key is to balance all three categories: product health, system health, and AI proxy metrics. A well-rounded OKR framework should include a North Star metric that captures the core value your product delivers, supported by other metrics that track specific aspects of performance.

In the rest of this chapter, we will discuss how to craft effective OKRs for your AI product, ensuring that your team focuses on what truly matters to drive success. We'll also explore examples of setting ambitious, user-focused objectives and defining measurable key results to monitor progress.

TYING METRICS TO GOALS

Having a well-defined set of goals is crucial for the success of any AI product. By understanding and leveraging the AI product metric blend, you can craft a holistic view of your product's performance and align it with user needs, technical excellence, and business goals. With this comprehensive framework, you'll be well prepared to measure success accurately and drive impactful product development. Let's now discuss building actionable OKRs that will help your team stay focused and aligned in this dynamic, AI-driven landscape.

OKRs represent your primary goal: the overarching objective you aim to achieve. It should be ambitious, inspirational, and aligned with the strategic vision of your AI product. You can have several OKRs, each addressing aspects of your AI product's development and performance. Each OKR consists of multiple KPIs or quantifiable metrics that communicate various dimensions of how well the product is performing relative to your OKRs. Your KPIs should be specific, measurable, achievable, relevant, and time bound (SMART). These indicators help track progress and determine whether you are on the right path to achieving your goal. Each objective should be comprehensive and aligned with the company's broader goals.

In "A Framework for Crafting AI Product OKRs", I'll share the framework I use for crafting OKRs for AI products. I like this framework because it provides a structured approach to setting and measuring goals. It emphasizes clarity, focus, and alignment with the product's core values.

The North Star metric represents the important KPI. It captures and represents the overall value your AI product is delivering. Each OKR can have multiple key metrics, depending on the complexity and scope of the objective. While the North Star metric represents the primary goal, other supporting KPIs can help measure progress in specific dimensions. Despite having multiple KPIs, each OKR should have only one North Star metric as a precise, focused measure of success that encapsulates the core value the product creates. It is the primary indicator of success for any OKR, reflecting the ultimate impact and progress.

A FRAMEWORK FOR CRAFTING AI PRODUCT OKRS

This framework incorporates a mix of metrics covered earlier in this chapter to provide a balanced and holistic view of progress and success. When crafting OKRs for AI products, you should include at least one metric from each metric bucket in the AI product metric cocktail: product health metrics, system health metrics, and AI proxy metrics. This framework helps maintain a structured and strategic approach to goal setting and performance measurement in AI product management. We always want to prioritize delivering impact and measurable value.

Having a reliable OKR framework can act as a foundation. For each AI product or feature, you'd fill in the framework with specifics relevant to your product. The examples provided are just illustrative. Adjust the framework as necessary based on the nuances of the AI product and your organization's strategic priorities. By integrating diverse metrics, you can craft well-rounded OKRs that drive your AI product's development and ensure its alignment with user needs, technical excellence, and business goals:

OKRs

Here you state the main goal for the next quarter. This should be user focused and explicitly stated (who is it for?) and needs to state the desired outcome (i.e., enhance the user experience by providing more personalized music recommendations).

Specific features

What features or changes will you introduce to achieve the objective?

North Star (KPI)

What is the primary metric showcasing product success? While this is typically a singular, focused metric, teams may use supporting metrics to provide additional context.

Product health metrics (Kpis)

Which metrics will measure user satisfaction or the product's health? Consider multiple relevant metrics such as retention rate, user satisfaction surveys, or feature adoption rates.

Guardrail metrics (Kpis)

What potential adverse side effects or risks do you want to monitor and minimize? Use a combination of metrics to track these risks effectively, such as error rates, response times, or user complaints.

System health metrics (KPIs)

How will you ensure that the tool or feature remains reliable and performant? Include multiple metrics to measure aspects such as system uptime, latency, or resource utilization.

AI proxy metrics (KPIs)

Which AI-specific metrics will you track to assess algorithm performance? Consider metrics such as model accuracy, precision, recall, or user engagement with AI-driven features.

Table 6-2 uses this framework to provide a detailed hypothetical OKR example for a streaming music service's recommendation system.

Table 6-2. Example OKRs for a streaming music service's recommendation system

Component	Example
Objective	Enhance the user experience by providing more personalized music recommendations.
Specific feature	Introduce three new personalization algorithms based on user behavior, mood, and music trends.
North Star metric (KPI)	Increase user engagement with recommended playlists by 25%.
Product health metric (KPI)	Reduce the number of users skipping songs within AI-generated playlists by 20%.
Guardrail metric (KPI)	Ensure that the overall time spent listening to the music does not decrease by more than 5%.
System health metric (KPI)	Maintain 99% system uptime, and reduce playlist loading times to under one second.
AI proxy metric (KPI)	Increase the precision of the recommendation algorithm by 15%.

Conclusion

Having a well-defined set of goals is essential for the success of any AI product. I hope the frameworks in this chapter for evaluating product success provide a structured approach to achieving your and your team's goals. There are always nuanced metrics that apply to specific situations, so it may take time to find the ones that work best for you and your team. That said, the framework for setting actionable goals and defining success will be similar across different projects.

Identifying the relevant metrics to add to your AI product metrics blend will help your teams capture a holistic view of the product's success. Defining specific objectives and OKRs can help AI teams focus on what truly matters and track their progress with precision. Identifying the right metrics and concentrating on a small set of crucial objectives will help teams maintain clarity and drive toward the most critical outcomes. Setting well-defined goals and measuring success accurately through a robust framework will drive progress and help align AI product development with broader business objectives. Using these frameworks will allow teams to understand and address the multifaceted nature of AI product performance.

In Chapter 7, I will cover the most popular product management tools I've come across as an AI product manager.

7

AI Tools for Product Managers

I was once asked whether AI will replace product managers. I responded by quoting (*https://oreil.ly/y1MZZ*) Harvard Business School professor Dr. Karim Lakhani: "AI won't replace humans—but humans with AI will replace humans without AI." In this instance, product managers will not be replaced by AI; product managers who don't leverage AI will be replaced by product managers who do.

In this chapter, I discuss the "AI-enhanced" type of AI PM and the AI tools that can enhance your craft if as one. A clarification: in recent conversations, I've noticed a common misconception—people often use the terms *AI product management* and *AI for product managers* interchangeably. While they might sound similar, these are two distinct concepts. Understanding the difference is crucial for grasping the broader landscape of AI's role in product development.

AI product management refers to the craft of creating AI products: products that are inherently powered by AI technologies. This role involves a deep collaboration with data scientists, ML engineers, designers, and other stakeholders to integrate AI into user experiences.

AI for product managers, on the other hand, refers to AI-enhanced PMs who can leverage AI to enhance their product management craft, whether they're working on an AI product or focusing on another (non-AI-powered product) area. These tools use AI to streamline various aspects of the product development lifecycle, such as sifting through vast amounts of market data to identify trends, or analyzing user feedback to highlight common pain points. This isn't about building AI into your product; it's about *using* AI to build a better product.

Tools to Enhance the AIPDL

Before we dive in, I should tell you that while I've mapped these tools to the different stages of the AIPDL where they can best help you, the mapping in Table 7-1 is just a guideline. Many of these tools are applicable in multiple stages of the AIPDL, and in some cases, the entire lifecycle. This framework is intended to give you a head start, but how you choose to leverage these tools will vary based on your workflow and evolving needs.

Additionally, each PM may have a completely different workflow, based on how they decide to incorporate AI into their work. These workflows evolve as new tools emerge and as advancements in AI provide new capabilities. Experimenting with different AI tools will allow you to craft a system that works best for you—and this system will likely change as you and the tools develop. While the following tools are among those that I recommend, there are others that I use throughout the AIPDL: for example, Google Gemini as a one-stop-shop tool and NotebookLM, which helps process large amounts of information and makes it more applicable to the use case I have in hand, i.e., adding as an input a two hour-long YouTube video and getting almost instantly the key points that are relevant to my work.

One word of caution: when using third-party AI tools, it's important to be mindful of the privacy and security of any confidential information you're sharing. Some of these tools might handle sensitive data, so it's always a good idea to consult with your company's privacy and legal teams to determine which tools are appropriate to use and which are not. Please note that the tooling landscape changes extremely fast. I update my newsletter (*https://marily.substack.com*) with the latest resources and tools.

Table 7-1. AI tools for each stage of the AIPDL

AIPDL stage	Tool	Description
Ideation	ChatPRD (https://www.chatprd.ai)	AI-powered brainstorming tool for generating product ideas and exploring early-stage concepts
	Gamma (https://gamma.app)	Interactive storytelling tool to help teams brainstorm and explore new product ideas
	Notion AI (https://oreil.ly/o4HHN)	AI-enhanced note-taking tool to organize, generate, and refine ideas during the early ideation stage
	Google Gemini Deep Research (https://oreil.ly/4zwN9)	Specialized version of Gemini for deep research tasks (by using Gemini Advanced)
Opportunity	Browse AI (https://www.browse.ai)	Web-scraping tool for gathering competitor insights, customer trends, and other valuable market data
	Komo (https://www.komo.ai)	AI-powered search engine that mines online communities for customer insights and helps identify market opportunities
	Perplexity (https://www.perplexity.ai)	AI tool for gathering competitive intelligence and validating product–market fit

AIPDL stage	Tool	Description
Concept/ prototype	Delibr AI (*https:// www.delibr.com*)	Facilitates repeatable workflows during product development, tracking iterations in concept and prototype stages
	Durable AI Site Builder (*https://durable.co*)	AI-powered website and app builder for creating digital products and prototypes quickly without coding
	Kraftful (*https:// www.kraftful.com*)	AI-powered feedback analysis for feature prioritization and product development
	Monterey AI (*https:// www.monterey.ai*)	Converts product requirements into workflows, helping PMs turn early concepts into practical prototypes
	Superhuman AI (*https://superhu man.com*)	AI-powered email management for improved collaboration and productivity during concept and prototyping phases
	Zeda.io (*https:// www.zeda.io*)	AI-driven road map builder that converts customer feedback into actionable features for product conceptualization
Testing/ analysis	Deepgram (*https:// www.deepgram.com*)	Converts speech in audio and video to text, aiding in transcription and testing for audio-focused products
	Fullstory (*https:// www.fullstory.com*)	Provides detailed insights into user behavior, helping PMs analyze product usability and pinpoint friction points during testing
	GrammarlyGO (*https:// oreil.ly/grammarly*)	AI-powered writing assistant to streamline content testing and analysis during product validation stages
	Optimizely (*https:// www.optimizely.com*)	A/B testing and experimentation platform for optimizing user experiences, useful during the validation and analysis phase

AIPDL stage	Tool	Description
Rollout	Durable AI Site Builder (*https://durable.co*)	AI site and app builder, helpful for deploying products and rolling them out to end users
	Fireflies AI (*https://fireflies.ai*)	AI meeting assistant for summarizing feedback and insights during the rollout process
	Tome (*https://tome.app*)	AI-powered tool for creating presentations and sharing product launch strategies

Tools for Collaboration and Tracking

As discussed in Chapter 4, maintaining close collaboration with your cross-functional teams and stakeholders is essential for ensuring alignment. To minimize risks and be set for success, it's crucial to figure out ways to collaborate efficiently with your partners. Here are some tools I have used in the past that help streamline communication, task tracking, and milestone management across *all* stages of the AIPDL:

Aha!
> Aha! (*https://www.aha.io*) is a road map software tool designed for product and strategic planning. It enables product managers to outline the product vision, strategy, and timeline, ensuring that all stakeholders are aligned on overarching goals. Aha! also offers scenario analysis, which allows you to plan for future challenges and explore alternative strategies, making it a powerful tool for navigating the uncertainty and complexity often inherent in AI product development.

Trello
> Trello (*https://trello.com*) is known for its simple UI and flexible, visual dashboards. It helps teams track tasks and assignments through customizable boards, lists, and cards, making it easy to adapt to the changing needs of AI projects. Trello's flexibility is particularly useful for AI PMs who need to manage multiple workflows and stakeholders, providing a clear overview of task progression and team responsibilities at every stage of development.

Jira

Jira (*https://oreil.ly/jira*) is one of the most widely used project management tools in software development, particularly for managing large, complex projects. It is favored by engineering teams for tracking bugs, issues, and feature development, making it a great fit for AI PMs who need to coordinate closely with engineering. Jira's robust reporting features provide detailed insights into project health, progress, and bottlenecks, making it a valuable tool for managing the intricate workflows involved in AI-driven products.

Productboard

Productboard (*https://oreil.ly/prdbrd*) goes beyond standard project management by integrating user insights, competitive research, and feedback from multiple channels into one platform. This tool allows product managers to evaluate and prioritize features based on business impact and customer needs. Productboard's impact scoring and timeline visualization capabilities help PMs make data-driven decisions while adjusting priorities in real time, ensuring that AI product development stays aligned with both user demands and business goals.

Each tool has its strengths, and your choice of which to use will depend on the specific needs of your product, organization, and team.

Conclusion

I've outlined how AI tools can empower product managers throughout the entire AIPDL, from ideation to rollout. These tools serve not only to streamline your workflows, but also to enhance decision making and drive strategic insights that would be impossible without AI. It's not about building AI into your products exclusively, but about using AI to amplify your own capabilities as a product manager. As the landscape of AI tools evolves, your role in product development will continue to expand, and those who leverage these tools effectively will stay ahead in an increasingly competitive market.

Before moving forward, remember that your workflows are personal. The tools presented in this chapter are just a starting point. Your unique work style, your company's structure, and the evolving nature of AI technology will continuously influence how you utilize these tools. And, as always, exercise caution when using third-party AI tools—always consult your company's privacy and security teams to ensure compliance.

Now, let's move on to Chapter 8, where we will explore the rise of AI agents—an entirely new frontier in AI product management. These agents have the potential not only to transform your product offerings, but to redefine the way you work, automating tasks, delivering personalized experiences, and creating new opportunities for innovation.

8

Building AI Agents

AI agents are fundamentally transforming industries by automating tasks, enhancing user experiences, and, most importantly, delivering on the promise that chatbots once made but never quite fulfilled. Researchers Poole and Mackworth discuss the foundational characteristics of an *intelligent* or *AI agent*. Their work introduces the framework depicted in Figure 8-1.

Within this framework, an agent is something that acts in an environment. An agent acts intelligently if:

- Its actions are appropriate for its goals and circumstances.

- It is flexible to changing environments and goals.

- It learns from experience.

- It makes appropriate choices given perceptual and computational limitations.[1]

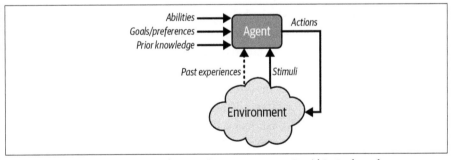

Figure 8-1. An agent interacting with an environment (source: David L. Poole and Alan K. Mackworth)

---

1 David L. Poole and Alan K. Mackworth, *Artificial Intelligence: Foundations of Computational Agents*, 2nd Edition (Cambridge University Press, 2017).

This model emphasizes the importance of adaptability and learning, which are critical features of modern AI agents. As shown in Figure 8-1, an agent's abilities, goals, and prior knowledge influence its actions within an environment. The agent senses stimuli, draws on past experiences, and uses its computational capacity to make decisions.

These intelligent systems have advanced far beyond simple conversational bots, and are now evolving into autonomous entities capable of not just understanding users' needs but *anticipating* them, executing complex tasks, and learning from each interaction. This progression is more than a technological shift; it is a strategic advantage that every forward-thinking product leader must embrace.

What Is an AI Agent?

AI agents are defined by their ability to perform autonomously, adapting and improving based on user interactions. Historically, AI agents began as rule-based systems—if you think back to early AI projects such as IBM's Deep Blue (*https://oreil.ly/1yuAV*) or even Google's AlphaGo (*https://oreil.ly/L7Ho1*), they were limited to solving highly specific problems, without much flexibility. Modern AI agents, however, possess a far greater degree of autonomy and learning capability, as evidenced by OpenAI's GPT-4–powered ChatGPT (*https://openai.com/gpt-4*), Google's Project Astra (*https://oreil.ly/JbIZR*), OpenAI's Operator (*https://oreil.ly/3Uqx1*), or Microsoft's Copilot (*https://oreil.ly/11zHZ*). These tools are not just reactive but proactive, enabling new levels of user engagement by predicting needs and even performing tasks on behalf of users.

OpenAI provides an option for its users to create their own custom agents, called *CustomGPTs*. These are tailored versions of OpenAI's GPT models designed to meet specific user needs or tasks. They don't require extensive fine-tuning of the base model or direct alterations to the model's underlying architecture. Instead, they focus on customizing behavior and outputs by using existing capabilities of the foundational GPT model in conjunction with dynamic prompts, tool integrations, and structured workflows.

I often get asked: "Wait, but isn't ChatGPT an AI agent?" The answer is no, not quite. ChatGPT is an impressive AI language model, but it's not classified as an AI agent. ChatGPT functions primarily as a conversational model—it responds to user prompts based on pretrained data, but it doesn't possess autonomy. It doesn't independently perform tasks or make decisions on behalf of the user. It needs explicit input, lacks a goal-driven framework, and doesn't act within an environment in an agentic sense.

However, custom Gems on Gemini or custom versions of ChatGPT (that combine instructions and extra knowledge/skills) can be considered AI agents, as they can autonomously execute tasks without constant and explicit user prompts. These tailored models are more autonomous and are designed to perform specific tasks, make decisions, and take actions, typically based on a user's needs. There are also ways for agents to interact with other tools or processes, offering more dynamic, proactive experiences and automated workflows via the use of, for example, zaps by Zapier.

In essence, *agentic products* are experiences that serve specific purposes; for example, NotebookLM is an agent that exists in order to understand complex topics and be a dedicated research assistant for the user. Agents operate based on predefined objectives, adapt to new information, and fulfill specific use cases. Kence Anderson captures the essence of agent autonomy in his book *Designing Autonomous AI* (O'Reilly, 2022), noting, "True autonomy in AI systems requires not just the ability to execute predefined tasks but the capacity to learn, adapt, and act independently in pursuit of user goals, often under dynamic and unpredictable conditions."

AI agents can:

- Help you plan, make decisions, and boost productivity
- Take action, create, and orchestrate tasks autonomously
- Make you feel connected, supported, and entertained
- Help you discover new information and learn
- Provide unique and personalized experiences tailored to the user and their goals

For product leaders, navigating the world of agentic products can feel new and, at times, overwhelming. Building AI agents requires a deep understanding not only of AI capabilities but also of your users' behaviors and needs. More than ever, your success relies on identifying the right opportunities to incorporate AI agents into your product ecosystem. The question is not just about whether to build an agent but about crafting the *right* agent—one that will meaningfully enhance user experiences while driving business value.

However, navigating this shift comes with challenges. Working with AI agents presents a host of considerations—from defining the scope of their autonomy to ensuring their ability to learn and adapt. They also require a different mindset in terms of product design: one in which the agent becomes an active participant in the user journey, rather than just a feature.

It's crucial to understand the evolving landscape of AI agents and their applications in real-world products. Companies such as Spotify are already using AI agents to provide music recommendations adapted to users' individual listening habits, while Amazon uses them for predictive inventory management and automated customer service, with a strong focus on learning from real-time data. Tesla is integrating AI agents into autonomous driving, while Apple is evolving Siri with advanced agentive capabilities. Studying the strategies of these early adopters can give product leaders a significant edge.

For those who can master these systems, the rewards are immense: reduced friction, better engagement, and even entirely new forms of value creation for users. In this chapter, I will guide you through the core concepts of AI agents, exploring the types of agents that exist today and how they differ from their predecessors. I will also examine how leading companies are leveraging these systems to create breakthrough products, and provide actionable steps for getting started with building AI agents for your own product. Whether you're new to this space or looking to refine your strategy, this chapter will equip you with the insights you need to succeed in the world of agentic AI products.

NOT JUST GLORIFIED CHATBOTS

At a glance, AI agents might seem like simply chatbots with a new name, but the reality is far more nuanced. While both AI agents and chatbots use NLP to engage with users, the scope, complexity, and capabilities of AI agents go far beyond what traditional chatbots offer.

Chatbots, as we've known them, are largely rule-based systems. They are designed to respond to a specific set of inputs based on scripted dialogues (e.g., "Where's my order?" or "When do you open?"). Think of the early iterations of customer service bots on websites such as Zendesk (*https://www.zendesk.com*) or the virtual assistants that helped users navigate simple transactions on Facebook Messenger.

AI agents, on the other hand, are designed to act autonomously, learn from interactions, and make decisions without relying solely on scripted responses. For example, while a chatbot might help you find a product on an ecommerce site, an AI agent like Amazon Alexa can anticipate when you'll run out of household supplies and automatically reorder them for you, based on historical purchase data. Moreover, AI agents can handle far more complex tasks, such as integrating with various external systems (APIs, databases) and autonomously optimizing their actions over time through mechanisms such as reinforcement learning.

Before discussing how to build an AI agent, let's take a look at how AI agents have evolved over the years.

EARLY RULE-BASED AGENTS

AI agents have evolved significantly from their early beginnings as rule-based systems to the more autonomous, adaptable models we see today. Early agents were limited by their rigid frameworks, programmed to perform specific tasks within controlled environments based on predefined instructions. They had little capacity for flexibility or learning, and were often constrained by the abilities and goals that were directly coded into them. A prime example is Microsoft's Clippy (*https://oreil.ly/zsxRn*), a little animated paperclip that appeared when a user was writing a document to offer assistance based on preprogrammed rules. While widely mocked by the world, Clippy was a glimpse into the future of AI agents.

Early strategy and simulation games provided a fascinating playground for AI agents, particularly these rule-based systems. For example, in the 1998 release of *Battle Chess* for MS-DOS (Figure 8-2), the pieces were controlled by simple AI agents with preprogrammed "move" and "capture" behaviors that followed the rules of chess. However, the AI had no capacity to adapt or learn from past games, relying solely on predefined strategies.

Figure 8-2. Battle Chess (MS-DOS, 1998)

In 1990s computer games like *Warcraft II: Tides of Darkness (https://oreil.ly/ EfhWt)* or *StarCraft (https://oreil.ly/6GUns)*, AI-controlled units patrolled designated areas, guarded critical resources, and engaged enemies using preprogrammed tactics. These games showcased early examples of AI-driven behavior, with enemy units responding dynamically to player actions, defending their bases, or coordinating attacks in a way that felt intentional and strategic. While this was a groundbreaking development for its time, the lack of adaptability was evident.

Another memorable game featuring early AI agents was *Lemmings* (1991). The game (Figure 8-3) had simple rule-based agents: the lemmings followed strict behavioral patterns, marching forward endlessly unless the player intervened to assign them a specific task, such as building bridges or digging. Again, these agents had no learning capabilities and could only follow a set path based on the player's inputs.

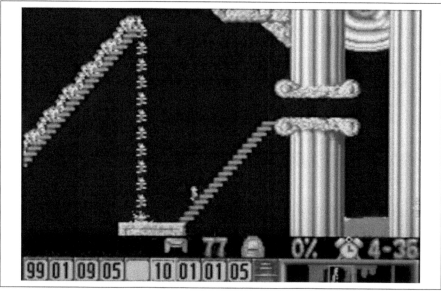

Figure 8-3. Lemmings (1991 "agents/bots")

These early AI systems set the stage for future developments by highlighting the limitations of purely rule-based approaches. Over time, AI agents became more dynamic and adaptable, evolving into systems capable of learning, making decisions, and taking actions autonomously.

The defining components of an agent are its:

Abilities
The tasks the agent can perform, such as speech recognition, decision making, or physical actions.

Goals or preferences
The agent's objectives or the specific desires it aims to fulfill. These are usually preprogrammed.

Prior knowledge
Information the agent already has about the environment or task.

Stimuli
Input from the environment, such as data from sensors, interactions, or user feedback. These inputs can include triggers that invoke specific behaviors based on predefined rules or logic. For instance, in simple systems, a particular sensor reading might directly activate a preset response (such as a thermostat turning on the heat when the temperature drops below a threshold). In more advanced AI agents, however, stimuli are processed dynamically, allowing the agent to adapt its actions based on prior experiences, goals, and contextual understanding. This evolution from rigid, rule-based reactions to adaptive, learning-based responses is a defining feature of modern AI agents.

Past experiences
The agent's history of interactions that shape future actions and decisions.

Over time, AI agents began to incorporate learning mechanisms, marking the shift from rigid, rule-based systems to more flexible, dynamic ones. The introduction of reinforcement learning allowed agents to learn from experience, adapting their behavior based on the outcomes of their actions. Agents no longer needed to be told what to do in every scenario. Instead, they could learn by trial and error, optimizing their actions to achieve goals.

For instance, in popular strategy games like 2010's *StarCraft II*, AI agents learn from their mistakes (*https://oreil.ly/OlDi3*), adjusting their strategies in real time based on the player's actions. These agents are designed to be more adaptable, using reinforcement learning to improve performance over time.

Today, AI agents incorporate deep learning and neural networks, enabling them to handle complex, multifaceted tasks with minimal human intervention.

These modern agents are not just limited to responding to immediate input; they can forecast, plan, and collaborate with other agents to achieve shared goals. They are still widely used in computer and console games such as *Red Dead Redemption 2, FIFA, Bioshock Infinite,* and *Grand Theft Auto V. Divinity: Original Sin II,* from 2017, also has an impressive non-player-character (NPC) AI.

One striking example is the rise of multi-agent systems. In environments such as healthcare, multiple AI agents collaborate *(https://oreil.ly/IdcZi)* to diagnose and treat patients, continuously learning and sharing information to improve outcomes. For instance, in one paper *(https://oreil.ly/gQTtY)* that created a hospital simulation for research purposes, different AI agents assumed the roles of doctors, nurses, and patients, collectively working toward better patient care (Figure 8-4).

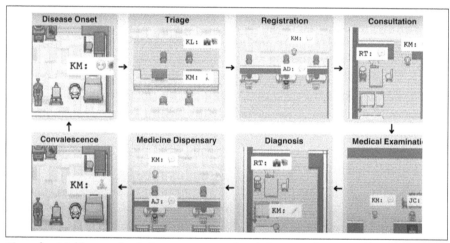

Figure 8-4. Multi-agent simulation system set at a hospital (source: https://oreil.ly/ziXvT)

These agents have memories, can take in sensory input, and can improve themselves based on new data. Their evolution has paved the way for sophisticated applications in areas such as autonomous driving, where vehicles (agents) interact with their environment, learn from real-time data, and make life-or-death decisions.

Agentive Products

Three major advancements have transformed AI agents into the sophisticated systems we see today: learning, decision making, and autonomous action. These advancements enable agents to process a diverse array of inputs, continuously adapt to their environment, and, most importantly, autonomously fulfill user needs without requiring explicit instructions:

Learning

Modern AI agents are designed to learn from experience, much like humans do.[2] This ability allows them to refine their behavior and improve their effectiveness over time. For example, a recommendation system in an ecommerce platform can analyze user preferences, purchasing patterns, and behaviors to make increasingly accurate suggestions. Through ML models, agents gain the ability to evolve their understanding of user interactions and environmental stimuli.[3]

Making decisions

As agents gather data and learn from their interactions, they also gain the ability to make informed decisions. This is not just about responding to stimuli with predefined actions; it involves evaluating multiple options and choosing the most appropriate response based on goals, constraints, and user needs. In the context of customer service, for instance, an AI agent might decide whether to escalate an issue to a human representative based on the complexity and sentiment of the conversation.

Taking autonomous action

The most significant leap in agents' evolution is their ability to act autonomously. These actions are not merely reactions to specific triggers; they are proactive decisions that reflect a deeper understanding of user intent. Autonomous agents can perform tasks such as scheduling meetings, sending notifications, and even generating creative content without direct human intervention. They act on behalf of users, anticipating their needs and optimizing outcomes with minimal input.[4]

Thanks to these advancements, AI agents have become indispensable in many applications. They provide personalized solutions by delivering the right response or action at precisely the right time. AI agents are no longer just

---

2 Tom M. Mitchell, *Machine Learning* (McGraw-Hill Education, 1997).

3 David Silver et al., "Mastering the Game of Go with Deep Neural Networks and Tree Search" (*https://oreil.ly/HLSwd*), *Nature* 529, no. 7587 (2016): 484–489.

4 Ahmed Elgammal et al., "CAN: Creative Adversarial Networks, Generating 'Art' by Learning About Styles and Deviating from Style Norms" (*https://oreil.ly/TlVr-*), *arXiv* preprint, arXiv:1706.07068, June 21, 2017.

bots performing repetitive tasks in isolation; they are integral parts of the user experience, designed to assist in meaningful ways.

For instance, users might employ an AI assistant to automate the process of organizing emails, setting up meetings, or even managing their lives (e.g., placing a grocery order). Creative professionals use AI tools to brainstorm ideas, design layouts, or even produce music.[5]

COMPARING CHATBOTS TO AI AGENTS AND MULTI-AGENTS

You might be wondering how exactly an AI agent differs from a chatbot, and what happens when multiple agents work together. While both chatbots and AI agents handle user interactions, their capabilities and autonomy levels are vastly different. To help clarify, I've broken down the key differences in Table 8-1 and Figure 8-5. This comparison highlights how they operate together, their unique capabilities, and the value they bring to different product scenarios.

Table 8-1. Comparing chatbots, AI agents, and multiple AI agents

Feature	Chatbot	AI agent	Multiple AI agents
Primary purpose	Conversation and basic task execution	Autonomous task execution and decision making	Collaborative problem-solving and task execution
Scope	Limited, often rule-based or predefined conversations	Broad, with complex tasks and adaptability	Complex, multistep tasks requiring teamwork and coordination
Autonomy	Low: Limited to predefined scripts and responses	Medium: Can make autonomous decisions and act on its own	High: Agents communicate, collaborate, and coordinate autonomously
Learning ability	Basic: Often relies on static rules or scripted responses	Advanced: Can use reinforcement learning and data feedback loops to adapt	Highly advanced: Agents learn both individually and as a group, improving coordination and performance

Feature	Chatbot	AI agent	Multiple AI agents
Interactivity	Primarily user facing; responds to user input	Interacts with both users and other systems	Interacts with multiple agents, users, and systems simultaneously
Complexity	Low: Simple logic or basic NLP models	Medium to high: Uses sophisticated AI models, can integrate multiple capabilities	Very high: Incorporates multiple agents with different specializations, requiring advanced coordination mechanisms
Decision making	None to limited: Follows scripted rules or decision trees	Autonomous: Can analyze data and make informed decisions	Collective: Makes decisions based on interagent communication and shared goals
Adaptability	Static: Limited to predefined changes in conversation flow	Dynamic: Can adapt to new information and changing environments	Highly dynamic: Agents adapt individually and collectively to optimize outcomes in real time
Example use cases	FAQ bots, basic reservations	Personal assistants, customer support	Autonomous driving (coordinated cars), virtual hospitals (AI agents collaborating on patient care)

Chatbots are primarily designed for conversation and basic task execution. They operate within a limited scope and with minimal autonomy, relying mostly on scripted responses. They are suitable for straightforward tasks such as FAQ interactions and making reservations.

In contrast, autonomous AI agents are capable of more complex and adaptive decision making, using advanced learning techniques such as reinforcement learning to improve their responses and actions over time. These agents are used in roles such as personal assistants and customer support, where a higher level of interaction and decision-making autonomy is beneficial.

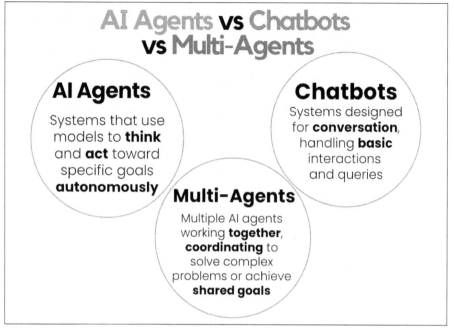

Figure 8-5. Comparison of AI agents, chatbots, and multi-agents (source: Dr. Marily Nika)

Multiple AI agents exhibit the highest level of complexity and dynamic interaction, collaborating and communicating to solve complicated, multistep tasks in real time. This type of AI system is used in highly coordinated environments such as autonomous driving and virtual hospitals, where seamless integration and collective decision making are crucial.

The differences in scope, complexity, and adaptability across these AI systems highlight the varying capabilities and suitable applications of each type of agent.

THE AI AGENT PRODUCT LANDSCAPE

The AI agent product landscape spans several domains, offering diverse tools that showcase how companies are leveraging AI to drive productivity and innovation. In the automation space, tools such as Magic Loops (*https://www.magicloops.ai*) and Respell (*https://www.respell.ai*) excel at streamlining repetitive workflows, from email management to creative content production, making them invaluable for businesses looking to enhance efficiency.

Virtual assistants form another prominent category, with examples such as Lindy (*https://www.lindy.ai*), which automates professional administrative tasks, and HyperWrite (*https://www.hyperwrite.ai*), a tool designed to support content creation and email management, boosting productivity for individual users and teams alike. For developers, specialized AI agents such as Sweep AI and Phind (*https://www.phind.com*) simplify coding tasks by automating bug fixes and providing efficient access to coding resources, empowering software professionals to work smarter.

Finally, new form factors such as Humane (*https://humane.com*) and Rewind (*https://www.rewind.ai*) integrate hardware with advanced AI capabilities, enabling seamless user experiences through voice-controlled and memory-enhancing technologies.

Because the AI space evolves quickly, many of these tools are likely to become outdated or be replaced by newer, more advanced agents. Some tools worth checking out are Cassidy (*https://www.cassidyai.com*) to build AI automations, CrewAI's Multi-Agent Platform (*https://www.crewai.com*), Criya (*https://www.criya.co*) for hyper-personalized campaigns, or Wayfound (*https://www.wayfound.ai*) for AI agent management. In my newsletter (*https://marily.sub stack.com*), I regularly share the latest trends and developments in the field.

As I write this in late 2024, Microsoft has deeply integrated its Copilot AI (*https://oreil.ly/11zHZ*) into its Office Suite and Windows, making it a core part of user workflows. Copilot assists with document creation, emails, and other tasks, and is positioned as a productivity AI agent available across devices.

In 2023, Meta built AI-driven personas (Figure 8-6), designed for social interactions, into Facebook and Instagram, though these are no longer used; Meta originally had plans to integrate them more widely into its Metaverse project, with its mixed-reality hardware.

I mention this because it was a good example of a strategic design choice that fostered personalization. The idea was that users could intuitively connect with the persona that best suited their needs, whether that was a playful creative assistant or a focused professional guide.

Figure 8-6. Meta's AI personas (no longer used)

In 2025, OpenAI introduced Operator (*https://oreil.ly/3Uqx1*), an AI agent designed to perform tasks autonomously within digital environments by leveraging a Computer-Using Agent (CUA) model. Unlike other agents that rely solely on APIs or structured inputs, Operator is equipped with GPT-4o's vision capabilities and can interact with interfaces by using a mouse and keyboard. This allows it to complete tasks such as filling out forms, navigating websites, and executing multistep workflows across various platforms (Figure 8-7).

Capabilities of OpenAI Operator include:

Dining and event planning
Book tables at restaurants, suggest highly rated venues, and secure tickets for events or shows.

Delivery tracking and scheduling
Monitor package deliveries, update schedules, and notify users of changes.

Travel and shopping assistance
Compare prices, make reservations, and provide updates on itineraries.

Human-agent collaboration

Users can intervene in ongoing tasks—such as modifying form inputs or verifying details—and return control to Operator, which seamlessly resumes its work.

Dynamic suggestions

Based on user behavior and preferences, Operator offers actionable recommendations, from curated news updates to meal ideas.

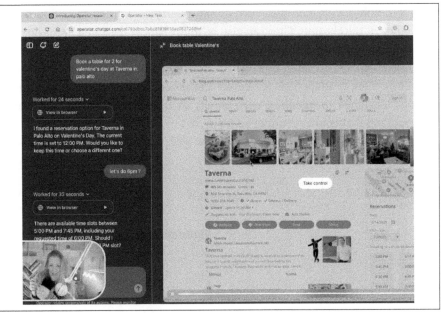

Figure 8-7. OpenAI's Operator in action: while making a restaurant reservation, it allows users to "take control" of the browser for manual input before seamlessly resuming automation

Crafting the Right AI Agent for Your Product

Now it's your turn. Start with your users' most urgent need. Choose a well-defined, specific use case. Focus on an area where AI can have the most immediate impact—whether that's automating customer service, streamlining internal processes, or enhancing user experiences. This section presents some considerations to help you figure out what type of agent can fulfill this need, and ends with a reflective questionnaire to help you put it all together.

TASK-SPECIFIC VERTICAL AGENTS VERSUS GENERAL-PURPOSE AGENTS

There are generally two categories of agents: task specific and general purpose.

Task-specific agents are designed for specialized tasks in specific domains, such as sending emails, booking tickets, or generating content; for example, an AI agent for a sales team that sends basic automated messages to prospects. These agents, called *simple reflex agents*, operate based on predefined if-then rules, reacting to specific stimuli without memory or learning.

Task-specific agents can be *goal based*—using AI to choose options that help them accomplish a specific goal, such as optimizing sales outreach or finding the most efficient travel route. They can also be *utility based*—designed to maximize a specific utility, such as minimizing energy consumption.

General-purpose or "all-in-one" AI agents have an internal model of the world that allows them to adapt their responses and actions to a changing environment. They are designed to handle a wide variety of tasks across multiple domains, from booking flights to generating content.

Figure 8-8 shows a framework I use to wrap my mind around the type of agent I will be building.

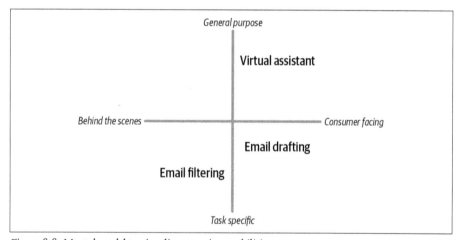

Figure 8-8. Mental model to visualize agentic capabilities

As you can see, another critical distinction of AI agents lies in whether they operate behind the scenes or are directly consumer facing. Understanding this contrast can help clarify the different roles agents play within a product ecosystem.

On the x-axis:

Behind-the-scenes agents

These agents work in the background, automating processes, optimizing operations, or managing workflows without direct user interaction. For instance, an AI agent embedded in a logistics platform may optimize inventory management or route planning, ensuring efficiency without the end user ever knowing it exists. These agents often focus on operational excellence, driving business outcomes through seamless integration with existing systems.

Consumer-facing agents

These agents interact directly with users, providing services, recommendations, or assistance in real time. Examples include virtual assistants such as Siri and Alexa, which engage users through NLP to fulfill tasks. These agents prioritize user experience, aiming to create intuitive and personalized interactions.

On the y-axis:

Task-specific agents

These agents are designed to handle highly specialized functions within a defined scope. They operate with a clear focus, addressing singular objectives such as email filtering, customer support, or scheduling. For example, Chatfuel (*https://chatfuel.com*) creates chatbots for customer interactions, while NotebookLM (*https://notebooklm.google*) serves as a personalized AI tool for summarizing and organizing notes, enabling users to quickly derive insights from structured documents. These agents excel at simplifying repetitive tasks or improving efficiency in targeted areas, making them ideal for organizations looking to automate specific workflows without requiring complex integrations.

General-purpose agents
These agents are versatile systems capable of managing a wide variety of tasks across multiple domains. Unlike task-specific agents, they adapt to dynamic user needs and handle diverse objectives, from generating content to managing workflows. Examples include LangChain (*https:// www.langchain.com*), a platform for integrating language models with APIs and databases, and Adept ACT-1 (*https://oreil.ly/act-1*), an AI agent designed to interact with software tools to help users accomplish tasks such as document editing and data analysis. These agents prioritize flexibility and scalability, making them powerful tools for businesses seeking to support broad use cases or deliver comprehensive solutions to users.

AGENT ACTIVATION

You need to decide how the agent will be activated. Agents can be proactive or reactive. Will it require user input via text, audio, or video, or will it act on its own? *Proactive agents* initiate interactions based on users' behavior or the context. Examples include Dynamic Yield (*https://oreil.ly/dyield*) and Zapier (*https://zapier.com*). *Reactive agents* respond only when a user explicitly invokes them. Examples include Botpress (*https://botpress.com*) and HubSpot's Chatbot Builder (*https://oreil.ly/SZoQq*). This choice depends on the user scenario and the level of interactivity needed for the task at hand. Understanding these factors ensures that your agent delivers value without feeling intrusive or overwhelming.

AUTONOMY

When designing an AI agent, it's crucial to consider what kind of autonomy is appropriate for your users. Agents can vary greatly in their level of autonomy (Figure 8-9). Some agents simply provide suggestions, while others can take action on behalf of the user—such as making purchases or scheduling appointments—with explicit consent. For example, an AI shopping agent may start by suggesting products but could eventually make purchases on the user's behalf, progressively gaining more autonomy. Controlling autonomy levels involves clear decision making about how much independence the agent should have. A critical choice is whether the agent acts reactively, requiring explicit user input, or proactively, anticipating user needs and initiating actions. For instance, a reactive agent might wait for a scheduling request, while a proactive agent could identify calendar conflicts and reschedule on its own.

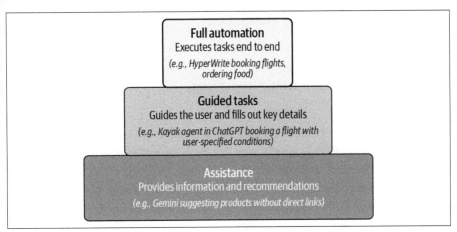

Figure 8-9. Agentic AI autonomy levels

FEEDBACK AND LEARNING

You'll also need to define your AI agent's long-term learning capabilities. Does the agent need to learn and adapt over time? Decide whether your agent will need reinforcement learning capabilities or feedback loops to improve its performance and responsiveness. You might also consider implementing user feedback tools, such as Zowie (*https://getzowie.com*) or Replika (*https://replika.com*), that allow users to "train" the agent through interactions. These loops can come from explicit feedback (thumbs up/down or star ratings) and implicit feedback (analyzing patterns in user interactions).

Designing these feedback mechanisms requires careful thought. To elicit user-driven feedback, you might implement tools that allow users to provide corrections or preferences directly, such as editing suggestions or flagging errors. For instance, a user might refine an AI-generated report or indicate that a recommendation wasn't relevant.

For system-driven feedback, you could enable the agent to analyze its own actions, learning from its successes and failures. Techniques such as reinforcement learning can help optimize future decisions based on outcomes.

Design Patterns for Agent Interaction

What will your agent *look* like? The UI and interaction patterns will also shape the overall experience. This section offers some design patterns to consider as you decide how users will interact with your agent.

SIDE PANEL

A persistent side panel offers a constant, accessible UI element that provides contextual assistance. This works well for both proactive and reactive agents, particularly in domains such as writing, sales, and productivity. A great example is Microsoft Copilot (*https://oreil.ly/11zHZ*) (Figure 8-10), which appears as a side panel in Microsoft Office applications, offering suggestions like rewriting content or creating charts based on user activities (online version available (*https://oreil.ly/ FyZHM*)). Similarly, HyperWrite (*https://www.hyperwriteai.com*) uses a side panel to assist with writing tasks by offering suggestions and content creation options.

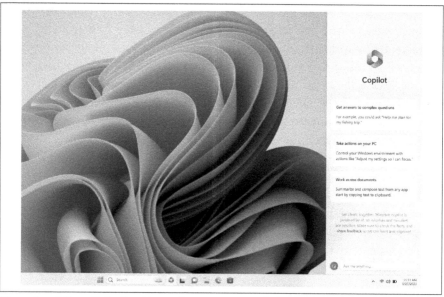

Figure 8-10. Microsoft Copilot side panel (source: Microsoft (https://oreil.ly/FyZHM))

FLOATING BUBBLE

A *floating bubble* is a small, movable icon that users can click to interact with the agent. It's often used in reactive agents that respond to specific user inputs. This pattern is commonly seen in tools like Intercom (*https://www.intercom.com*) or Floatbot.AI (*https://floatbot.ai*) (Figure 8-11), where the bubble allows users to easily access chat-based assistance.

Figure 8-11. Intercom (A) and Floatbot.AI (B)

CHAT INTERFACE

A dedicated conversational space, either through text or voice, is ideal for all-in-one agents. This approach provides users with a direct way to communicate with the agent and is most useful for handling more complex tasks. Salesloft (*https://oreil.ly/-A2J-*), for instance, uses this format to facilitate conversational interactions between users and AI agents for customer support or sales inquiries (Figure 8-12).

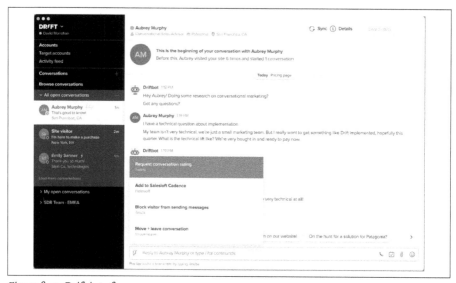

Figure 8-12. Drift interface

INTEGRATED UI

In this design, the agent is seamlessly integrated into the product's workflow, offering suggestions or actions without requiring a dedicated interface. This is ideal for proactive agents that subtly enhance user interactions without demanding direct engagement. Two examples are Grammarly, which acts as a real-time assistant by analyzing text, suggesting corrections, and improving writing style dynamically, and Tesla's Autopilot, an advanced AI agent capable of analyzing real-time data to make autonomous decisions while driving.

POP-UP NOTIFICATIONS

Pop-up notifications are best suited for proactive agents that need to guide users or provide timely advice. These notifications can alert users of opportunities or actions the agent can take based on their behavior. For example, Grammarly (Figure 8-13) uses this approach to suggest grammar improvements or rewording in real time, ensuring that users receive relevant advice just when they need it.

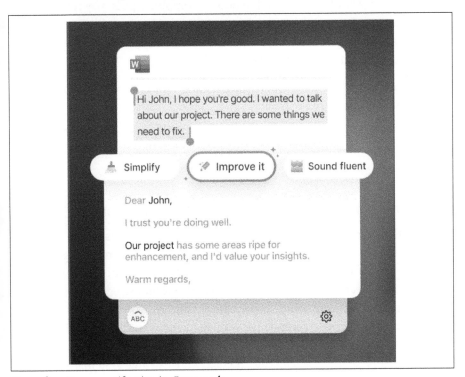

Figure 8-13. Pop-up notification in Grammarly

COLLABORATIVE BROWSER INTERFACE

OpenAI's Operator introduces a unique *collaborative browser interface*, blending autonomous action with manual control to create a flexible and user-friendly experience. This interface allows users to interact directly with tasks being performed by the agent, such as filling out forms, navigating websites, or booking services. Unlike traditional interfaces that rely solely on either automation or user input, Operator's design facilitates a seamless transition between both modes.

For instance, when making a restaurant reservation, Operator autonomously navigates to a reservation platform, selects appropriate options, and prepares the booking. At any point, users can choose to "take control" of the browser to manually adjust details, as shown in Figure 8-7—such as selecting a different time or verifying specific inputs—before returning control to Operator, which resumes the task without disruption. This capability ensures accuracy and adaptability, particularly in tasks where user preferences or complex inputs may require manual intervention.

The collaborative browser interface excels in situations requiring a combination of automation and human oversight, such as:

- Comparing ticket prices across platforms while allowing users to view and select their preferred options

- Completing online applications with user-specified customizations

- Reviewing and approving actions before submission, ensuring confidence in automated workflows

SCALABILITY, FUTURE-PROOFING, AND OTHER CONSIDERATIONS

It's likely that, over time, your agent will need to scale up. Consider how your AI agent can handle increased user load, expand to include different languages, or integrate new features over time. Think about the backend infrastructure needed to support scaling and real-time responses to user questions.

Data privacy is paramount, especially if your AI agent handles sensitive user information. Ensure compliance with regulations such as GDPR and the California Consumer Privacy Act (CCPA).

Also ensure that the agent can interact with existing systems, APIs, and databases within your organization. Compatibility with CRM, enterprise resource planning (ERP), or customer service platforms might be essential. Platforms can help integrate the agent consistently across tools. I recommend MuleSoft (*https://www.mulesoft.com*) for API integrations and Make (*https://oreil.ly/cab_B*) for process automation.

Define Success for Your Agent

At the end of the day, an agentic AI product is still a product, so the metrics you learned about in Chapter 6 apply. Consider using these metrics to evaluate your agent:

Task completion rate
How effective is the agent in fulfilling its intended tasks? Example metrics include the number of successful scheduled meetings or the response rate to automated messages.

Accuracy and quality
Can the agent handle complex user queries? Feedback mechanisms, such as thumbs up/down or star ratings, can help assess the quality of interactions.

Intervention
Does the user escalate to a human often? Track the number of sessions in which human intervention was needed, with success meaning a decreasing need for these interventions over time.

Satisfaction
Implement surveys or feedback forms to capture direct user feedback. Positive comments on usefulness, ease of interaction, and the agent's ability to assist with tasks are great indicators of success.

AI Agent Questionnaire

Use this questionnaire to help you and your team think through the decisions you'll need to make as you design your agent:

- What user need will your product fulfill?

- Will your agent be task specific or general? If task specific, will it be a simple reflex agent, goal based, or utility based?

- Will your agent be proactive or reactive? If reactive, how will users invoke it?

- Does the agent need to learn and adapt over time? Decide whether your agent will need reinforcement learning capabilities or feedback loops to improve its performance and responsiveness.

- Will you implement user feedback tools that allow users to "train" the agent through interactions? If so, which one(s)?

- What should the experience look like?

- Which design pattern(s) will your agent use for user interaction?
- How will the agent scale? What infrastructure will you need?
- What data does the agent access, and how will you secure it?
- How will the agent personalize the user experience?
- How will the agent integrate with other tools or platforms?
- What metrics will you use to define success?

Conclusion

AI agents are not just a technological marvel; they represent a new paradigm in how we solve problems, interact with users, and design products. Throughout this chapter, we've explored the evolution of AI agents, from simple rule-based systems to the complex, learning-driven entities that shape our digital experiences today. We dove into crafting AI agents tailored to specific product needs and outlined a practical checklist to help you make informed decisions. Whether your goal is to automate tasks, enhance personalization, or empower users to make decisions autonomously, the possibilities are endless.

But this is just the beginning. The role of an AI PM is to keep learning, keep iterating, and stay ahead of emerging trends. As AI continues to evolve, so too will the tools and strategies we use to bring these intelligent systems to life. You've now explored the foundational principles of AI product management—how AI fits into the broader product lifecycle, how to measure success, and how to create meaningful, scalable AI experiences.

For more real-world examples, certifications, and up-to-date content, I invite you to visit AI Product Hub (*https://www.aiproduct.com*) for ongoing insights, resources, and community-driven discussions to ensure that your journey into AI product management remains dynamic and impactful.

Appendix

Product Review Template

Here you can find the template for your product review to ensure that all critical aspects of a decision are carefully evaluated. Make sure to include clear recommendations, consider all trade-offs, and outline key steps for implementation. You can find more information on product reviews in Chapter 3:

Executive summary
    A brief summary of the decision that needs to be made.

Solution space
    Key options being considered, with pros, cons, and trade-offs.

Factor	Option A	Option B
Factor 1	+ + − −	+ + − −
Factor 2	+ + − −	+ + − −
Factor x	+ + − −	+ + − −

Scope of the review

What outcome is expected from the review; for example, a decision, discussion, or just alignment.

Background

Brief background on the topic, with relevant documents and impact.

Key stakeholders

Who is involved, affected, or responsible for the recommendation.

Question in hand and recommendation

Clearly state the question and provide a well-supported recommendation.

Metrics or evidence supporting recommendation

Key KPIs/OKRs or insights that validate the recommendation.

Risks and mitigation

Possible risks and how they can be addressed.

Implementation considerations

Next steps for acting on the recommendation.

Lessons learned (optional)

Insights from previous reviews of this process for future improvements.

AI Product Requirements Document Template

Here is a template for structuring your AI PRD. Make sure to clearly define the problem space, outline user needs, and demonstrate how AI will uniquely solve these challenges. This will help align teams and ensure a well thought-out vision for execution:

Your product's name (PRD)

Author: Marily Nika

Contributors:

When building an AI product, remember to have an answer to the question: *"How can we use AI to help our users?"*

Relevant Documents

1. About

Elaborate on the high-level problem space. What is the tl;dr of what you are trying to achieve? Frame the problem space.

2. Market Insights

Explain the market: Is it saturated? Are there many organizations working on similar problems?

— Customer Segments

Who are your users? If you don't know, which users will you target as per the hypotheses you will be making?

— User Personas

Create an archetype of a user—a one-size-fits-all persona that you will be solving for. What AI-specific solutions are they leveraging?

— Market Analysis

— Competitor Analysis

— Technology Analysis

3. The Problem

— Use Cases

What are your users trying to achieve? Provide a list with details.

— Pain Points

Why can they not achieve their goals? If they can achieve their goals, what is problematic about the way they are going about achieving them?

— Problem Statement

Write the full problem statement in a format such as: <Athletic John spends too much time trying to figure out the right fitness and nutrition routine for himself, and he never achieves his performance goals>

It's a good practice here to mention why AI is uniquely positioned to solve this problem.

— Hypotheses and Mission Statement

What is your main hypothesis for this work? By bringing x to life, <you will be making z easier/more efficient/more fun/more personable, and so on, for the user>.

4. The Solution

- Ideation

  List of all ideas/features that could solve the prioritized pain point(s).

- Leveraging AI

  Why is AI appropriate or essential for the solution(s) you will be developing?

- Feature Prioritization

  Use the RICE framework (Table A-1) to prioritize your features and solutions.

- AI MVP

  Will you be training a model as part of the MVP? Will this be a hybrid solution? Give a brief, high-level explanation of how your model will work, what techniques you will be using, and what data might be required.

- Road Map

  Create the prioritized road map.

- Technical Architecture

  Provide a high-level overview of the AI product's technical architecture, including the hardware, software, and infrastructure required for its operation. Please note, you just need to provide this on a very high level (client, server, where does data flow from/to?). The software engineers/scientists will then create a design doc.

- Assumptions and Constraints

  Make a list of any assumptions made during the development process, as well as any constraints that may limit the AI product's functionality or performance.

- Risks

  Describe potential risks associated with the AI product's development and deployment, along with strategies for mitigating those risks.

5. Requirements

— User Journeys

— Functional Requirements

This is a deeper dive into the product's functionality and how it will work, including high-level technical specifications and algorithms. Don't talk about what kinds of algorithms the scientists will use; instead, talk about why you need algorithms and what smart functionalities they will support.

— Nonfunctional Requirements

Give a list of requirements that do not relate to the product's core functionality, such as security, scalability, performance, and usability.

— AI and Data Requirements

Describe the data sources and types of data required for the AI product to function effectively, as well as any data collection or management processes.

6. Challenges

Will you have enough data? How do you plan to acquire it? Do you have enough funds for it? Do you have enough user conviction that what you are bringing to life will indeed solve your users' problems?

7. Positioning

Table A-2 gives you a compact snapshot of your product for executive slides.

8. Measuring Success

— Metrics

How will you measure success for the overall product? (Use generic PM metrics such as engagement, retention, and so on.)

— AI-Specific Metrics

What does quality mean to you, from a strategic perspective? How will you measure success for the model? What quality is good enough to launch? What AI-specific metrics will you use? What does quality mean to you?

— What is your North Star metric?

9. Launching

— Stakeholders and Communication

Make a plan for how stakeholders and users will be kept informed of the AI product's development and any changes to its functionality or performance.

— Rollout Strategy

Are there any strategic considerations for going to market?

What is your rollout plan?

Table A-1. The RICE framework

Feature	Reach 1–100% of your target user persona	Impact (1–10)	Confidence (1–10)	Effort (1–10)	Score (R × I × C) / E
Personalized recommendation for YouTube channel	100%	7	5	8	

Table A-2. Snapshot of product

Use case	Pain point	Possible solutions	Impact of solution

Visit the AI Product Hub (*https://oreil.ly/yx4xn*) for more templates and frameworks.

Worksheet 1: Assessing AI Opportunity for Your Organization

This worksheet will help you systematically evaluate AI opportunities for your organization, as discussed in Chapter 5. Start with Section 1 to assess which AI capabilities are most relevant to your business, then work through subsequent sections to develop a comprehensive view of how AI could fit into your organization.

For the capabilities assessment ("Section 1: AI Capabilities Assessment"):

- Rate impact from 1 (lowest) to 5 (highest).
- List concrete use cases specific to your business.
- Be honest about implementation challenges.
- Consider both technical and organizational factors.

For remaining sections:

- Be specific and quantitative where possible.
- Include input from different departments.
- Focus on business value, not just technical feasibility.
- Document assumptions and uncertainties.

Work through this with key stakeholders including:

- Product/engineering leads
- Business stakeholders
- Technical experts
- End users (if possible)

SECTION 1: AI CAPABILITIES ASSESSMENT

Rate each capability's potential impact (1–5) and note specific use cases for your business (Table A-3).

Table A-3. Capabilities assessment

Capability	Impact (1–5)	Potential use cases	Implementation challenges
Learning from data			
Personalization			

Capability	Impact (1–5)	Potential use cases	Implementation challenges
Content generation			
Distillation/summarization			
Prediction/forecasting			
Real-time adaptation			
Workflow automation			
Creative collaboration			
Interactive spaces			
Error detection			

SECTION 2: COMPANY MISSION AND AI ALIGNMENT

1. What are your company's core goals or mission statements?

_____

_____

_____

2. How can AI contribute to achieving these goals?

_____

_____

_____

3. What specific problems in your business could AI solve?

_____

_____

_____

SECTION 3: PRODUCT PAIN POINTS

1. What are the top challenges faced by your current products or services?

_____

_____

_____

2. Which user segment would benefit most from AI integration, and how?

_____

_____

_____

3. What specific AI capabilities could address these pain points?

_____

_____

_____

SECTION 4: USER IMPACT

1. How will AI improve the overall user experience?

_____

_____

_____

2. Which KPIs could AI enhance?

_____

_____

_____

3. Could AI make your product more accessible or inclusive? How?

_____

_____

_____

SECTION 5: BENEFITS AND RISKS ANALYSIS

1. What are the top benefits of integrating AI?

_____

_____

_____

2. What are the potential downsides?

_____

_____

_____

3. Rank the importance (High/Medium/Low):
  – Benefit 1:

  _____ (_____)
  – Benefit 2:

  _____ (_____)
  – Downside 1:

  _____ (_____)
  – Downside 2:

  _____ (_____)

SECTION 6: RESOURCE ASSESSMENT

1. What AI resources does your company currently have?
  – Talent:

  _____
  – Infrastructure:

  _____
  – Expertise:

  _____

2. Are these sufficient for long-term maintenance? ☐ Yes ☐ No
  If no, what's needed?

  _____

SECTION 7: COMPETITIVE ANALYSIS

1. How are competitors using AI in their products?

_____

_____

_____

2. What competitive advantages could AI provide?

_____

_____

_____

3. Is AI adoption urgent in your market? Why?

_____

_____

_____

SECTION 8: IMPLEMENTATION DECISION

1. Should you proceed with AI integration? ☐ Yes ☐ No

2. Build in-house or outsource? Why?
 — Strategy: _____
 — Reasoning: _____

NEXT STEPS

1. Implementation timeline: _____

2. Key stakeholders: _____

3. Success metrics: _____

4. Resource allocation: _____

Worksheet 2: AI Implementation Strategy Worksheet

Here is a worksheet that will help you evaluate whether and how to integrate AI into your product, as discussed in Chapter 6. It's meant to be filled out collaboratively with your product team and key stakeholders. The goal is to think through all aspects of AI implementation, from core metrics to user impact to resource requirements.

Take your time with each section. It's better to identify potential issues now than to discover them after implementation. Don't worry if you can't fill out every field; use this as a living document that evolves as you learn more.

Consider revisiting this worksheet:

- When planning new AI features
- During quarterly planning
- Before major infrastructure changes
- When evaluating build versus buy decisions

Tips:

- Be specific in your metrics; avoid vague goals.
- Consider both positive and negative impacts.
- Think about long-term maintenance, not just initial launch.
- Include diverse perspectives from your team.

SECTION 1: CORE PROJECT COMPONENTS

Objective: What is the main user-focused goal for the next quarter?

_____

_____

Specific features: What features or changes will you introduce?

_____

_____

North Star metric (KPI): What is the primary metric that showcases success?

_____

_____

Product health metrics: List metrics measuring user satisfaction/product health.

1. _____

2. _____

3. _____

Guardrail metrics: What risks or adverse effects will you monitor?

1. _____

2. _____

3. _____

System health metrics: What indicates reliable and performant operation?

1. _____

2. _____

AI proxy metrics: What AI-specific metrics will you track?

1. _____

2. _____

SECTION 2: USER IMPACT ASSESSMENT

How will AI improve the overall user experience?

_____

_____

Which KPIs could AI enhance?

_____

_____

How could AI make your product more accessible/inclusive?

_____

_____

SECTION 3: BENEFITS AND RISKS ANALYSIS

Top benefits:

1. _____

2. _____

Potential downsides:

1. _____

2. _____

Priority ranking (circle one for each):

- Benefit 1: High / Medium / Low
- Benefit 2: High / Medium / Low
- Downside 1: High / Medium / Low
- Downside 2: High / Medium / Low

SECTION 4: RESOURCE ASSESSMENT

Current AI resources:

- Talent:

  _____

- Infrastructure:

  _____

- Expertise:

  _____

Sufficient for long-term maintenance? ☐ Yes ☐ No
If no, what's needed?

_____

SECTION 5: COMPETITIVE ANALYSIS

How are competitors using AI?

_____

_____

What competitive advantages could AI provide?

_____

_____

Is AI adoption urgent in your market? Why?

_____

_____

SECTION 6: IMPLEMENTATION DECISION

Should you proceed with AI integration? ☐ Yes ☐ No
Build in-house or outsource? Why?

- Strategy: _____
- Reasoning: _____

Index

About the Author

Dr. Marily Nika is a GenAI product lead at Google, one of the world's foremost AI educators, and a founder of the AI Product Academy (*https://www.aiproduct.acad emy*), which has awarded more than 10,000 certifications. With a PhD in computer science and more than 13 years of experience building AI products at Google and Meta, she brings deep expertise and insight to the field.

Based in Silicon Valley, Dr. Nika was named Amplitude's "Best Product Industry Influencer" in 2024 and has been featured in *Fortune*'s "40 Under 40," *TechCrunch, TED AI, The Guardian*, and more. She is also a Harvard Business School Fellow, author, and TEDx speaker. Through her writing on AI product management at Substack (*https://marily.substack.com*) and LinkedIn (reaching approximately 150,000 readers), Dr. Nika shares valuable insights on the future of AI. Additionally, she is the founder of the AI PM Bootcamp (*https:// maven.com/marily-nika/ai-pm-bootcamp*) and a cofounder of the AI Product Hub (*https://www.aiproduct.com*), a global platform dedicated to educating, connecting, and empowering AI builders worldwide.

Colophon

The cover illustration is by Susan Thompson. The cover fonts are Guardian Sans Condensed-Medium and Gilroy Semibold. The text fonts are Minion Pro and Scala Pro; the heading font is Benton Sans.

O'REILLY®

Learn from experts.
Become one yourself.

60,000+ titles | Live events with experts
Role-based courses | Interactive learning
Certification preparation

 **Try the O'Reilly learning platform
free for 10 days.**